The Internet and Email for
the Over|50s

Image credits

The Internet and Email for the Over 50s

Bob Reeves

For UK order enquiries: please contact Bookpoint Ltd, 130 Milton Park, Abingdon, Oxon OX14 4SB. Telephone: +44 (0) 1235 827720. Fax: +44 (0) 1235 400454. Lines are open 09.00–17.00, Monday to Saturday, with a 24-hour message answering service. Details about our titles and how to order are available at www.teachyourself.com

For USA order enquiries: please contact McGraw-Hill Customer Services, PO Box 545, Blacklick, OH 43004-0545, USA. Telephone: 1-800-722-4726. Fax: 1-614-755-5645.

For Canada order enquiries: please contact McGraw-Hill Ryerson Ltd, 300 Water St, Whitby, Ontario L1N 9B6, Canada. Telephone: 905 430 5000. Fax: 905 430 5020.

Long renowned as the authoritative source for self-guided learning – with more than 50 million copies sold worldwide – the Teach Yourself series includes over 500 titles in the fields of languages, crafts, hobbies, business, computing and education.

British Library Cataloguing in Publication Data: a catalogue record for this title is available from the British Library.

Library of Congress Catalog Card Number: on file.

First published in UK 2007 by Hodder Education, part of Hachette UK, 338 Euston Road, London NW1 3BH.

First published in US 2007 by The McGraw-Hill Companies, Inc.

This edition published 2010.

The Teach Yourself name is a registered trade mark of Hodder Headline.

Typeset by MPS Limited, A Macmillan Company.

Printed in Great Britain for Hodder Education, an Hachette UK Company, 338 Euston Road, London NW1 3BH, by CPI Cox & Wyman, Reading, Berkshire RG1 8EX.

The publisher has used its best endeavours to ensure that the URLs for external websites referred to in this book are correct and active at the time of going to press. However, the publisher and the author have no responsibility for the websites and can make no guarantee that a site will remain live or that the content will remain relevant, decent or appropriate.

Hachette UK's policy is to use papers that are natural, renewable and recyclable products and made from wood grown in sustainable forests. The logging and manufacturing processes are expected to conform to the environmental regulations of the country of origin.

Impression number   10 9 8 7 6 5 4 3 2 1

Year   2014 2013 2012 2011 2010

Contents

Welcome to *Teach Yourself Internet and Email for the Over 50s.*

I've written this book for the more mature newcomer who wants to get to grips with the Internet and email. I've assumed no prior knowledge of using a computer, and tried to keep jargon to a minimum. Where I have had to use any, the word is highlighted in **bold**, and you will find it in the 'jargon-busting' glossary at the back of the book.

You can work your way through the chapters in order or you can dip into the bits you are interested in. Before you dip in, if you are a complete novice user I'd recommend that you first read through:

Chapters 1 to 4, which cover general computing basics.

Chapters 9–10, which cover the basics of using the Internet.

Some of the chapters share common themes so you might want to work through those in sequence:

Chapter 5–8 cover all aspects of email.

Chapters 11–14 are related to additional ways of communicating with others using the Internet.

Chapters 15 and 16 are about Internet safety.

Chapters 17–25 cover using the Internet for everything from shopping to dating and pretty much anything else you can think of.

Once you have developed the basic skills of searching the Internet and finding your way around websites, you will soon be able to find anything you want on the Internet even if the topic you are interested in isn't covered specifically in this book. There are hints and tips throughout the chapters to help you on your way.

The book assumes that you have a Windows 7 computer. The main program that it covers is Internet Explorer 8, which will be already present on your computer. Any other programs referred to are either already installed or are freely available from the Internet.

Finally, when you first start, computers can be a bit scary. One mature night class student said to me that the computer screen is so cluttered it looks like a flight deck on an aeroplane with little buttons and signs all over the place. However, the big difference is that if you go wrong on the computer, it doesn't matter. Your computer is virtually impossible to break – so don't be scared of it, just click away and see what happens. Have fun.

If you are looking for a more general introduction to all aspects of computing you might also be interested in *Confident Computing for the Over 50s* also in the Teach Yourself series

Bob Reeves

About the author

Bob Reeves has been working with computers for the last 25 years. He started his career in one of the country's leading financial services companies involved in IT and training roles. He later retrained as a teacher specializing in business and ICT. He has taught thousands of children and adults on a range of business and ICT courses over the years with students as young as 4 and as old as 80.

Bob has worked on a number of projects here and abroad related to computer education and has written for a number of computer publications. He has also written several textbooks on ICT including the best-selling *Computing for the Over 50s* also available in the Teach Yourself series.

Bob is married with two grown-up sons. He says that his wife has been his most difficult student to date and his two sons both chose careers that had nothing to do with computers.

Only got one minute?

There's been something of a computing revolution going on in the last 20 years. If you've picked this book up, it's probably because you want to join the revolution! There has never been a better time.

The Internet is a global connection of computers. Anyone with a computer and an Internet Service Provider (ISP) like Tiscali or BT can connect into it and become part of a massive network of millions of people all over the world.

The Internet is made up of millions of pages of information in the form of websites. There are websites for everything you can think of from day-to-day tasks like shopping and banking through to more exciting past-times like tracing your family tree or even finding a new partner!

The skills needed to access all of this information are relatively simple. A few carefully chosen words typed into a 'search engine' like Google and the ability to spot a link on a web page (the pointer changes shape!) and you will be 'surfing the Net' in no time.

Email or electronic mail allows you communicate with people all around the world. Using email is a bit like sending a letter, except you don't have to post it and it will arrive almost instantly. All you need is the address of the person you want to send it to and an email provider like Hotmail or Google Mail. Email is free and you can access it from any computer that is attached to the Internet.

You will soon find that a few skills learnt on the computer will take you a long way.

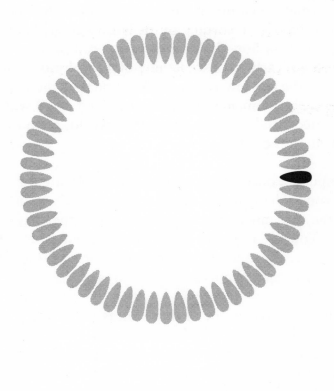

5 Only got five minutes?

In a world full of computer whizz kids it's easy to forget that anyone over the age of about 40 did not receive any formal education in computers and IT when they were at school. According to the latest figures, over 70 per cent of households now own a computer so there has clearly been something of a revolution going on over the last few years. At the same time there has been the phenomenon of the Internet and email with an estimated 1 billion users around the world, 50 million of them in the UK.

Computers, once the domain of the 'nerds' are for everyone. That's not to say that they are easy to use, but they are much easier to use now than they have ever been. You will also find that there are a few core skills that can really take you a long way. Also, skills learned in one area can be applied to new areas.

'Surfing the Net' is one of those phrases that you hear bandied about. The Internet (or Net) is a global connection of computers and anyone with a computer is allowed to join in. One of the key uses of the Internet is the World Wide Web or simply the Web. You have probably seen addresses for websites, most of which start with the www.

The Web has billions of web pages full of information but the key to accessing all of this information is actually quite simple. Using web browser software such as Internet Explorer, which you will already have on your computer, you can access a 'search engine' such as Google. Using a few carefully chosen search words you can very quickly find what you are looking for.

Websites are a collection of individual web pages. Once you are inside a website you will find that there are common ways of moving around so that you can access even more information. Web pages are linked together using 'hyperlinks' or 'links' for short. You will know when you are on a hyperlink because the mouse pointer changes shape. When you click on the link it will take you off to another page and so on and so on.

Many people and organizations make websites for various reasons. For many businesses it is a key way of marketing and selling products and services. This can be of great benefit to us as consumers as prices are often lower on the Internet. Many government organizations and charities also use the Net as do many individuals. This means that in amongst all the good websites there is a lot of rubbish and you need to know how to filter out or avoid it.

Email or electronic mail is the computer equivalent of sending a letter. Once you are on the Internet you can send and receive emails, which get delivered almost instantly. You need to know the address of the person that you want to send the email to. These are in the format glynishubblethwaite@hotmail.co.uk where the bit before the @ is the name of the person and the bit after is the name of the email provider on the Internet.

Using email software you can send messages and other information. For example, you might have some holiday photographs that you want to send to someone. Rather than posting them you can attach them to the email and the recipient can see them straight away.

You can also use your computer to make telephone calls over the Internet. The beauty of this is that it is totally free and you can even see the person you are talking to.

The Internet and email have revolutionized the way that we communicate. We have many ways of keeping in touch with friends and family wherever they live in the world. In addition, the Internet can be used to make new friends and get involved in new social networks. You might ever only meet some of these people 'online' or the friendship might spill over into the real world.

The range and choice of what you can do with the Internet and email is probably only limited by your imagination.

1

Choosing a computer

In this chapter you will learn
- *what the main parts of the computer are*
- *how to understand a computer specification*
- *how to choose an ISP and what connection speed to go for*
- *how to make your decision of what to buy and where to buy it*

1.1 The computer system

When you buy a computer the manufacturer will publish the specification of the computer. A basic **computer system** is made up of the base unit, sometimes called a tower, a screen, keyboard, mouse and printer. Computer equipment such as this is called **hardware**.

You will also need what is called **software**. This refers to the programs that you will run on the computer. Programs are needed to let you do all the things you want to do like send emails and get onto the Internet.

The price of the computer is usually based on how fast it works and how much information you want to keep on it.

1.2 What you will need

The base unit or tower is where all the clever stuff goes on. The main features to look for when you are choosing your computer are:

Processor
The processor is the brains of the computer. Everything that is done on the computer goes through the processor. The speed is measured in gigahertz (GHz). The simple rule is the higher the number of GHz, the faster your computer will work. Anything over 2GHz is perfectly adequate for most computer users.

Memory

This is sometimes called RAM (random access memory). This is measured in gigabtyes (GB). The simple rule here is the higher the number of GB, the faster your computer will run. 2GB of memory is the minimum recommended when running Windows 7 – more is better.

Hints and tips

How important is speed? All modern computers are fast. Most things you do on the computer such as typing documents, surfing the Internet, emailing, etc. do not require a really fast processor or lots of memory. If you plan to use your computer for playing computer games or editing movies, then faster processor speeds and more memory might be needed.

Hard disk drive (HDD)

This is the amount of information that the computer can store. This is measured in gigabtyes (GB) and, you guessed it – the bigger the number, the more information it will store. Anything over 100GB is more than adequate for most computer users.

CD or DVD drive

These are the trays on the front of the tower that slide out so that you can put in a CD or DVD. CDs and DVDs have all sorts of information on them including computer programs, data and films. It is recommended that you get a DVD drive as these will cope with CDs and DVDs. A CD drive will cope only with CDs. It is recommended to get a DVD-R or DVD RW, which means you can save information onto DVDs as well as take information off them.

Hints and tips

Computer manufacturers bring out new computers all the time. They are always bringing out faster processors and increased memory. This means that your computer will start to become out of date quite quickly. This does not really matter for most users.

Monitor

This is the screen on which everything is displayed. As with the computer tower, there are thousands of variations to choose from. All new monitors now are flat, which means that they take up only a small amount of space on your desk. The main decision is about the size of the screen. The size is measured in inches. Standard sizes are from 15 to 19 inches. Bigger screens are more expensive but are much easier to read. The best advice is to go to a shop and have a look at the different sizes.

Keyboard and mouse

You don't usually get much choice with these as your computer will come with a standard keyboard and mouse. All keyboards are pretty much the same and you use them for typing in letters and numbers. The mouse is a pointing device. You point at things on the screen and click the buttons to make things happen. If you don't like wires everywhere, you can invest in a wireless mouse.

Printer

This is for producing printed copies of anything you do on your computer. As with everything else to do with computers, there are thousands to choose from. The main decisions are whether you want an inkjet or a laser printer and whether you want colour or just black and white prints. Inkjets are usually cheaper to buy, but the ink cartridges can run out quickly and are expensive to replace. Laser printers are slightly more expensive to buy, produce slightly better quality and print more quickly.

Colour printing is more expensive than black and white printing as you have to buy colour cartridges as well as black ones. However, unless the only thing you will be doing is typing documents, then a colour printer is going to be essential.

An inkjet printer.

1.3 The operating system (Windows 7)

You will also need to choose what software you want.
When you buy your hardware, you usually get some
software with it. There is more on this in Chapter 3, but
at this stage you must make sure that the computer you
buy comes with an operating system. This is a program
that enables your computer to work and is essential.
The most common operating system is Microsoft
Windows®, which normally comes as part of the price
of the computer. Make sure any computer you choose
has this on it already.

Hints and tips

Several different versions of Windows have
appeared over time. Most new computers come
with Windows 7 Home Premium or Professional.
Either of these is fine.

1.4 Plugging things in using USB ports

In the next chapter, you will learn about a range of additional devices that can be plugged into your computer. Most of these devices attach using a USB connection. Make sure your computer has got at least six USB ports. This will allow up to six different devices to be plugged in at the same time.

USB ports.

1.5 Connecting to the Internet

If you want to connect to the Internet you will need a modem or router. This is a device that might be built into the computer, or may be plugged into the back. You have to choose which company to get your Internet connection from, for example Tiscali, BT, AOL, etc. and they will normally supply you with a modem or router to plug into one of the USB ports. The other end plugs into the telephone socket. If you have broadband, you will also be supplied with filters, which you need to plug into those other phone sockets to which telephones will be attached. These enable you to make phone calls while using the Internet at the same time.

You might like to consider have a wireless router. As the name suggests, this means that you do not have to physically plug your computer in as the information will travel wirelessly. Your Internet access will be a bit slower than plugging in with a wire but it does mean that you can have your computer anywhere in the house and you will still be able to get access to the Internet without having to trail wire around all over the place.

These days, broadband is available in most areas. Broadband means that the access to all of the information is quite quick. Without broadband, access is boringly slow.

A wireless routes.

1.6 Internet connection speeds

When you are choosing your ISP you need to look at the 'connection speeds' that they offer. This refers to how quickly the information on the Internet will appear on your screen. Connection speeds are measured in **Megabits per second (Mbs)**. The higher the number, the faster you will be able to get information from the Internet. Typical connection speeds are anywhere between half a megabit (usually called 512K), all the way up to 20Mbits. In some areas you will not be able to get very high speed connections and you might not have any choice but 512K or 1Mb is sufficient for many uses such as reading emails and general browsing. However, if you can get a faster connection you are advised to do so.

Hints and tips

Ask your friends and relatives which ISP they use. Go on recommendation if you can.

1.7 Where to get your computer from

As you will discover when you try to buy a computer, there are several different manufacturers to choose from and you can buy from a range of places. Generally speaking, you get what you pay for and it pays to shop around.

- *High Street chains: These are quite competitive on price and have a good selection of computers. They are a safe bet if you don't have a good local specialist.*
- *Specialist computer shops: The level of advice you get will probably be a lot better in a specialist computer shop, though they may not be able to be as competitive on price. They are usually good at looking after you if you have any problems later. It's good if you can find one that comes recommended.*
- *The Internet/mail order: You can get some real bargains from catalogues and the Internet (if you have access). Internet and mail order businesses don't have the overheads that the shops do and this is how they can do it cheaper. The disadvantage is that you won't get to see the computer 'in the flesh' before you buy it. Use a bigger company that you have heard of or that has been recommended. You could always find the computer you want in a shop and then see if you can get the same thing cheaper on the Internet.*

Most new computers come with at least one year's warranty although this can be extended to three. Most warranties require the computer to be sent to the manufacturer, which means you will be without it for a week or so.

IMPORTANT THINGS TO REMEMBER FROM THIS CHAPTER

1 *Processor speed is one of the key factors in how fast your computer will work. It is measured in Gigahertz (GHz).*

2 *Memory (or RAM) is another key factor that determines how quickly your computer will work. This is measured in Gigabytes (Gb).*

3 *The hard disk is where all information is stored. This is also measured in Gigabytes (Gb).*

4 *Your computer should have a CD or DVD drive. If choosing just one go for a DVD-RW as this will cope with CDs and DVDs.*

5 *Monitors are measured in inches across the diagonal face. 17–19 inches is common although you might like to pay extra for a bigger one.*

6 *There are two main types of printer: inkjet and laser. You can get these in either mono (black and white) or colour.*

7 *Windows 7 is an operating system. It is a package of software that controls all aspects of the computer.*

8 *If you are buying a computer make sure it has lots of USB ports – at least six if possible.*

9 *You will need a modem or router to get onto the Internet. Connection speeds vary between 512Kb and 20Mb.*

10 *If you are buying a computer, think about where you will be using it as it may be a good idea to get a laptop, which is portable.*

2

Other equipment you might need

In this chapter you will learn
- *what other computer equipment you might need*
- *what specification of equipment is needed*

2.1 What peripherals do you need?

Many of the peripherals that you can buy have quite
specific functions, so it is not worth investing in them
unless you have good reason to do so. Most devices
these days plug into your computer using a USB
connection and your computer should have at least
six USB ports for you to plug in to.

Hints and tips

Most devices are now 'plug and play', which
means that when you plug them in, the computer
spots that they have been plugged in and they will
work automatically.

DIGITAL CAMERA

These are now more common than old-fashioned cameras. They do not use film. Instead, they store the image electronically on a card that slots into the camera. You can store hundreds of images on a card and can transfer the images onto your computer where you can store and print them.

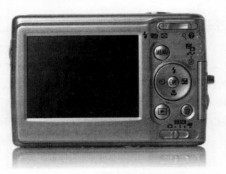

The main things to look for when buying a digital camera are:

▶ *Megapixels: This refers to the number of tiny dots used to make up the image. The larger the number of megapixels, the better clarity you get in your finished photographs. Anything over 8 megapixels is adequate for the average photographer.*

▶ *Optical and digital zoom: This refers to the amount of magnification you can get, i.e. how far you can focus in on images that are far away. Optical zoom is better as it is achieved using the camera's lens;*

3.3 optical zoom is usually sufficient. Digital zoom digitally zooms in on the image; 6 digital zoom is perfectly adequate.

▶ *LCD: This is the small screen that you use to preview the image. The size is measured in inches; 2.5 inches is adequate although larger screens are easier to see.*

Hints and tips

You can also buy digital camcorders, which you can use to record moving images. Like a digital camera, you can transfer the images onto your computer where you can watch the film you have made.

WEB CAM

This is a camera that you place on top of your screen, which takes moving pictures of you! The idea of this is that you can contact people using your computer and they can see and hear you while you are talking to them. If they have a web cam at their end, you can see them too. These are particularly useful if you have friends in other countries that you would like to see and hear, rather than just write to. Choose one that has a resolution of 640 × 480 or higher. The higher the resolution, the clearer the images will be. If you want to be heard, you will need a web cam with a built-in microphone.

A web cam.

SCANNER

A scanner is a device that works a bit like a photocopier. You put the document or picture onto its glass surface and by scanning it, you create a computerized version

A scanner.

of the document or picture. This is particularly useful if you have old photographs that you would like to put onto the computer. Scanners can also be used to scan any other kind of document as long as it is A4 size or less. If you do get a scanner, make sure it has at least 4800dpi. This is dots per inch. The higher the number, the clearer the scanned images will be.

MEMORY STICK

These are small storage devices that let you store information in a portable way. If you ever need to move information from one computer to another, then you will need a memory stick. These are sometimes called flash memory or flash drives. They are very small and plug into the USB port. You can copy information onto them and then take them with you. For example, if you go to an evening class and want to take in some work that you did on your home computer, then you can use a memory stick. The amount that a memory stick can store is measured in gigabytes (GB). The price of these has come down massively over the last few years and a 1GB stick will only cost you a few pounds so you might as well buy one with lots of memory on it.

A memory stick.

SPEAKERS

These are just the same as the speakers on your stereo or radio except you plug them into the back of your computer. You will need speakers if you want to play music or videos, or if you want to talk to other people over the Internet, for example, using a web cam. Speakers that plug into the electricity supply can deliver more volume if needed, though those that draw their power through the USB ports are often loud enough. The amount of volume you can get is measured in watts (W). More watts mean more volume.

CD/DVD BURNER

This allows you to make your own CDs or DVDs. There are many different formats of CD and DVD. A standard CD or DVD drive will allow you to read information from the disk, but not to put any information back onto it. You might want to be able to create (burn) your own CDs and DVDs. For example, if you take lots of photographs, you could burn them onto a CD to give to family and friends. If you have made a film using a digital camcorder, you might want to burn it onto a DVD. If you think you might want to do this, then you should make sure that you get a CD-R, CD-RW or DVD-R or DVD-RW. The R means recordable and the RW means re-writable. You can buy some that plug into a USB port or you can buy a computer that already has one built into your base unit/tower.

Hints and tips

Although we tend to associate DVDs with films, they are actually used to store any kind of information (films, music, photographs, documents, etc.). DVDs can store much more information than a CD so it is best to get a DVD drive.

IMPORTANT THINGS TO REMEMBER FROM THIS CHAPTER

1 *'Peripherals' is the general term used for additional devices that you can plug into your computer.*

2 *You can copy images off a digital camera to be stored and viewed on your computer.*

3 *You can connect a web cam, which allows you to send still or moving images of yourself to someone on another computer.*

4 *A scanner can be used to create digitized images of photographs or other paper-based images and documents.*

5 *Memory sticks are small devices that plug into your USB ports and can be used to transfer information from one computer to another.*

6 *Speakers are needed to hear any kind of audio including music or voice, for example, when making a phone call over the Internet.*

7 *If speakers plug into the mains supply, the sound can be amplified much better than if they take their power from the computer.*

8 *If you computer has a CD-R, CD-R, DVD-R or DVD-RW, it is capable of copying information onto CDs and DVDs.*

9 *The R stands for Recordable, which means that information can be recorded onto them but only once.*

10 *The RW stands for Rewritable and means that they can be used over and over again to store information.*

3

Programs (software) you might need

In this chapter you will learn
- *what a computer program is*
- *which computer programs are essential*
- *what computer programs you might need*
- *about software versions*
- *about software that comes with devices*
- *about free software*
- *about licences*

3.1 What software do you need?

Software allows you to do the things you want to do. Without software, you can't do anything with your computer – it is just a pile of useless equipment. There are different types of software, each of which allows you to carry out different jobs on your computer. You may have heard of some already. For example: word processing software is needed to type letters and other types of documents; web browser software is needed to access the Internet; email software is needed to send and receive emails.

Some of the biggest businesses in the world are involved in making and selling software. It is a very competitive market, and these companies are always trying to get you to use their software. You may have heard of some of them, for example, Microsoft and Google. This chapter will look at some of the most common brand name software available.

Microsoft
Microsoft is the biggest name in standard software. Its owner, Bill Gates, is one of the richest men in the world. Microsoft is responsible for Word, Excel, PowerPoint, Access, Publisher, Internet Explorer, Outlook and Hotmail, which are some of the most common software used. They also make Windows. Now you can see why he's one of the richest men in the world!

Internet Explorer
This is called a **browser** and is needed to view all of the information on the Internet. Internet Explorer (IE) is usually found on any computer that has Windows on it – so you have probably already got it. The latest version is called Internet Explorer 8 and we will be using it in this book.

Email
Most email software is web-based. This means that you do not need to buy it as you can use it for free on the

Internet. Another advantage of web-based software is that you can use it from anyone's computer – you do not have to use your own. You will get free email from the company that you get your Internet from, known as your Internet Service Provider (ISP).

Internet Service Provider (ISP)

This is a service that gives you access to the Internet. It is basically a telephone service that allows you to get Internet access down your telephone line. This service is provided by a business, e.g. BT, NTL, Talk Talk, etc. To get on the Internet, you must have an ISP. There are lots to choose from and they vary in price and the speed at which they work. It is a competitive business so it is worth shopping around and asking family and friends which one they use and whether they are happy with it. If you live in a cable TV area you can get a deal where TV, telephone and Internet is all available through cable at a fixed price per month.

Anti-virus

This software stops your computer getting infected with computer viruses. Viruses are small programs written by people with nothing better to do. They attack your computer and can damage it or the information that is on it. Anti-virus software searches your computer for viruses and kills them. If you buy anti-virus software you are entitled to updates, which means that you will get new versions of the software that will kill any new viruses.

Anti spyware/adware software: Spyware and adware is software that installs itself on your computer without you knowing it, when you are in the Internet. It tracks what you do on the computer. The information is usually used for marketing purposes. So you might get lots of junk email (called **spam**), or lots of windows popping up trying to sell you something. These are called **pop-ups**. Anti spyware/adware software gets rid of it. Make sure that your anti-virus software also gets rid of spyware and adware.

Media Player: If you want to view videos and films, or listen to music you will need a media player. These are usually free and the most common ones are Windows Media Player, which is part of Windows 7, or Real Player. These will open up automatically whenever you try to play music or view a video or film. Some websites use their own media players e.g. the BBC website use iPlayer.

Hints and tips

If you are buying a new computer, you should ask your computer shop to put all of the software on the computer for you. This will save you a job.

3.2 Software Versions

The businesses that make software are forever bringing out new versions. This means that they have added some new features to the software. Some of these new features are genuinely useful. You have to pay to **upgrade** to these new versions, and it is not always worth it.

When they bring out a new version, sometimes the screens look different and this can be very disconcerting or confusing. For example, Internet Explorer 8 looked a bit different from Internet Explorer 7. However, you should find that the new version will do everything that the old version did, and some new stuff too.

Is the upgrade necessary?

It is not essential that you upgrade to the latest version of everything. If you are happy with the version you are using then you can stick with it.

3.3 Software supplied with devices

Whenever you buy a new device such as a digital camera or a webcam, it will come with a CD or DVD that contains the software for the device. All devices need software to make them work on your computer. The software also includes useful functions. For example, the software that comes with your digital camera will allow you to **browse** and edit your photographs on-screen. The problem with all this software is that it is all different. For example, the software supplied with a Canon camera will be different to that supplied with a Kodak camera.

Having said that, most software conforms to some standard rules, as you will see later. All software should also be supplied with a user manual to help you get started.

3.4 Free software

Generally speaking, you get what you pay for and this is also the case with free software! There is a lot of free software available on the Internet for you to download. If you buy a computer magazine, you often get a CD packed with free software. Some of this is genuinely good stuff. For example, software companies often give away older versions of their software to encourage you to buy the latest version. Some free software is only free for 30 days and then you have to buy it – so watch out for this. It will normally just run out after the 30 days without causing any problems. Some free software is free because it's rubbish.

As a rule, it is recommended that you only put free software onto your computer if you think you will be using it. The temptation is to clutter up your computer with all of this stuff because it is free. However, every time you add something to your computer, it does alter the settings, which might cause problems elsewhere. Also, you will end up with a long list of programs making it harder to find the ones you do want to use.

3.5 Licences

Finally, make sure that any free software you use is genuine. It is very easy to create copies of software and you may know people who offer you 'free' software.

It is illegal to use software that you have not paid for. When you buy legitimate software you get a licence to use it on your computer. In theory, you can be heavily fined for using unlicensed software.

Make sure that you keep the original packaging of all software that you buy, as this is the licence. This also means making sure that you get a copy of Windows from whomever you buy your computer from.

IMPORTANT THINGS TO REMEMBER FROM THIS CHAPTER

1 *Software is also referred to as 'programs' or 'applications'.*

2 *Software is what you actually use your computer for. For example, you need software to write letters, send email or surf the Internet.*

3 *Internet Explorer enables you to get onto the Internet. You will also need an Internet Service Provider (ISP) to provide you with a connection.*

4 *Email software allows you to send and receive emails. There are free email services on the Internet.*

5 *You should get some anti-virus software on your computer so that it is less likely to get damaged by a computer virus.*

6 *Spyware and adware are a bit like viruses and you don't really want them on your computer so you should install software that checks for them gets rid of them.*

7 *Media player software allows you to listen to music and watch video. Windows Media Player comes as standard with Windows 7 and other players are available free on the Internet.*

8 *When you buy peripherals for your computer they normally come with their own software, which you have to install.*

9 *Free software is available on the Internet and some of it is very good.*

10 *Microsoft Windows is not free and you should never use illegal copies. All software is supplied with a licence that proves that you have paid for a legitimate copy.*

4

Getting started on your computer

In this chapter you will learn
- *how to switch your computer on and off*
- *how to use the mouse and keyboard*
- *about the Windows desktop*
- *how to open and close programs*
- *how to open and close folders*

4.1 Switching the computer on and off

To switch your computer on, you need to find the button that has this symbol on it.

This is the on/off button although you should normally only use it to switch the computer on.

Press the on/off button and release – and wait.

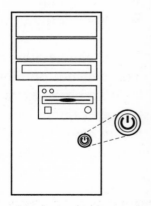

The computer will now go through a start-up routine that may take a few minutes. If nothing appears on the screen, it may be that the monitor is not switched on. The monitor also has an on/off switch, so make sure that this is on. You can tell that the computer and monitor are on as there is a small (usually green) light that will light up when they are on.

Hints and tips

The start-up routine is carried out by the Windows operating system that we talked about in Chapter 1. It has to go through this routine every time you switch on. Windows will also switch the computer off when you tell it to, which is why you never need to use the on/off button to switch your computer off.

If it is a brand new computer, you will probably be prompted to set up a name and password for it. If this is the case, give it a sensible name (your own name for example) and a password that you will remember. It might be worth writing this down somewhere safe. When it has finished its routine, you will see the Windows desktop, which will look something like this:

There may be other windows open on your desktop. This depends on how the computer has been set up. If you do have extra options other than those shown in our example, don't worry. You can ignore them for now and you will soon discover how to close any windows that you don't want.

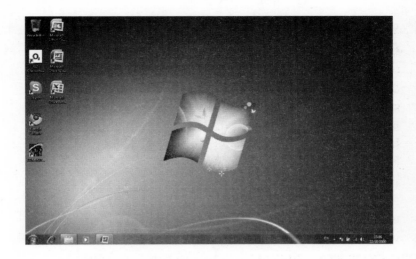

Think of the desktop like a normal desktop – a flat surface with lots of things on it. You will always start at the desktop and will use it a lot, so you need to get used to it. The small pictures you can see are called icons. By double clicking (see below) on these with the mouse, you can open up programs and folders.

Also, note the Windows icon in the very bottom left-hand corner. This is referred to as the Start button and it opens a menu which will provide access to everything on your computer.

The Windows desktop can be customized. You can move the icons around and add your own background, called 'wallpaper'. You can also add 'gadgets' such as a clock or a calendar. This means that your desktop might not look exactly the same as the one shown here.

4.2 Using the mouse

To make things happen, you can either use the mouse or the keyboard. Your mouse will have at least two buttons called the left and right buttons. It may also have a scroll wheel between the two buttons.

As you move the mouse around on your mouse mat, it will move a small pointer on the screen. All programs work with a mouse – you simply point and then click on the icons and menus that you want to use.

Throughout this book, when you need to click on something on the screen, it will be shown in the text in single speech marks. For example, if you need to click on a menu on the screen called Save, the instruction will read either: Click 'Save' or Select 'Save'.

To use the mouse:

1 *Hold it lightly using the thumb on one side and your third and little fingers on the other. This leaves your first and second fingers free for clicking and using the scroll wheel. You might want to practise moving the mouse around and watching as the pointer moves.*
2 *As well as pushing the mouse around, you will also need to lift it slightly from time to time. The mouse only works if it is flat on your mouse mat, but*

sometimes you simply run out of mouse mat! When this happens, you need to lift the mouse off the mat and reposition it in the centre of the mouse mat before you start moving it again. This might be a bit tricky when you first start, so have a play until you feel more comfortable with it.

Hints and tips

Some mice are more sensitive than others, which means that the pointer will move by different amounts. If you use more than one computer, it might take a while to get used to a different mouse.

You can actually move the pointer all the way across the screen without having to move the mouse much at all using the lifting technique described here.

4.3 Clicking on things

There are three types of click:

▶ *A left click (known as a click). This is used mainly when you want to select something from a list or menu.*
▶ *A double left click (known as a double click). This is another thing that you might need to practise when you start. A double click is when you click twice on the left button, quite quickly. You use this when you click on icons.*

▶ *A right click. This provides access to hidden menus. Right clicks work only in certain places, as you will start to discover later.*

Let's practise the clicks now.

1 *First, from the desktop, click (that's a single left click) on the Windows icon in the very bottom left-hand corner.*

2 *Click on 'Documents'. This will then show a window that looks a bit like the one below. It is called a window because it opens in a frame. Don't worry if yours does not have exactly the same number of little yellow folders and icons in as this.*

You will notice that there are three small icons in the top right-hand corner of the window. These are displayed in every window in every program.

The first one is called Minimize. This closes the window but leaves it available so that you can get it back later.

3 *Click on the 'Minimize' icon. The window closes, but if you look at the bar across the bottom of the*

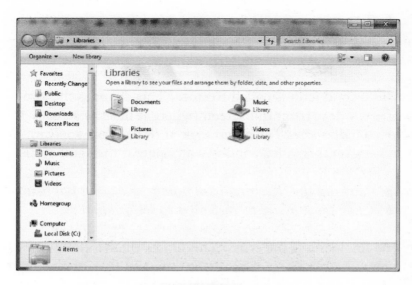

screen (called the Taskbar), it is still available here. Any windows that you minimize will have a small icon in the Taskbar which you can click on to get it back to full screen. This feature is useful as it means you can have lots of different things open at the same time, and you can use the Taskbar to get to them quickly. If you hold your mouse over each icon, it will show a thumbnail view of that window to remind you what it is.

4 *To re-open the 'Documents' window, click on the Windows Explorer icon now from the Taskbar at the bottom of the screen.*

The second icon is called Restore. This changes the size of a window from full screen (where it fills the screen) to a smaller size. The advantage of this is that you can have several smaller windows all open at the same time.

5 *Click on the 'Restore' icon now to see what happens.*
6 *Click on it again to restore it to its original size.*

The final icon is the cross. This closes the window. You will use this a lot as this is the main way of closing things down when you have finished with them.

To close this window:

7 *Click on the little cross in the very top right-hand corner of the window as shown.*

You have used a double click and a click to open and close a window. You are now back at the desktop.
8 *Move the mouse pointer somewhere on the desktop where there are no icons.*
9 *Right click. A hidden menu is displayed. This menu will be different depending on where you press the right click.*

10 *Click somewhere else on the desktop and the hidden menu will disappear again.*

Hints and tips

The scroll wheel comes in handy when you are looking at things that take up more than a screenful. In this case you have to move up and down, and you can use the scroll wheel for this.

4.4 Using the keyboard

This is a bit more straightforward as it works in the same way as a typewriter. That is, you press the keys and whatever you type will appear on the screen.

When you are on the desktop you don't really need to type anything, but you will use it a lot in other programs. There are a few keys on the keyboard that carry out specific functions. You will be introduced to these as you need them, but it is worth pointing a few out now.

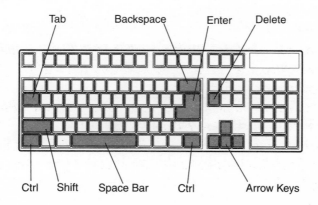

Throughout this book, when you need to press one of the keys on the keyboard, the name of that key will be shown in capitals. For example, if you need to press the ENTER key, the instructions will read: Press ENTER.

- ▶ *ENTER: You will use this key a lot. It is used to tell the computer you want to do something and is used when typing to start new lines.*
- ▶ *SPACE: The space bar is used to add spaces in between words when typing.*
- ▶ *TAB: This is really useful when you are filling in forms when you are on the Internet. It will move you from one part of the form to the next and saves you having to click.*
- ▶ *SHIFT: Allows you to type capitals and gives you access to all of the characters displayed at the top of the keys, for example, above the numbers.*
- ▶ *CTRL: Can be used for shortcuts. These are ways of doing things quicker. You will be told about these as you work through the book.*
- ▶ *BACKSPACE and DELETE: Used a lot when typing. They delete (erase) any characters that you have typed incorrectly.*
- ▶ *ARROW KEYS: Can be used like the mouse to move the pointer on the screen around (in some programs).*

4.5 Opening and closing programs

Programs are all of those things that you use your computer for, for example, word processing, or surfing the Internet. To do these things, you have to open the appropriate program. You open programs from the desktop in one of two ways:

▶ *Double click on the icon that represents the program on the desktop.*
▶ *Click on 'Start' (the windows icon in the very bottom left-hand corner).*
▶ *Click on 'All programs', find the program on the list and click on it.*

Hints and tips

All programs have little pictures associated with them. These are called icons. For example, Microsoft Word has a blue W and Internet Explorer has a blue E. There is also a label with the icon that tells you what program it is.

It is easiest to open programs from an icon, but sometimes the icon does not exist, so you have to go through the Start menu. To practise, we are going to open Microsoft Word. To open from an icon:

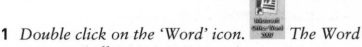

1 *Double click on the 'Word' icon.* The Word program will open (see page 42).
2 *To close the program, click on the small cross in the top right-hand corner of the window.*

To open from the Start menu:

1 *Click on the Start button.*
2 *Move the mouse pointer to 'All Programs'. A list will now be displayed.*
3 *Find 'Microsoft Word' in the list and click on it. You may have to click on the option for Microsoft Office in the list first if you can't find it. The program will load.*
4 *Click on the cross to close the program.*

The process of opening and closing any program is exactly the same. This means there will always be either an icon, or if there is no icon, the name of the program will appear on the list in the Start menu. All programs can be closed by clicking on the cross in the top right-hand corner.

4.6 Opening and closing folders

Folders are where you save your work. When you first start off there are four libraries containing folders. These libraries are called Documents, Music, Pictures and Video and are organized like this to make it easier to find what you are looking for. Think of folders like normal paper folders. They are just somewhere to put your work. All work (whatever it is) is stored in files. We will start in a folder called Documents which at first will have nothing in it.

Hints and tips

It might help to think of your computer as an electronic filing cabinet. The folders are where you will store all of your work.

Folders have their own icon, which is a little yellow folder! Whenever you see a little yellow folder, it means that there is some work stored in it. Later on, you will make your own folders.

As a practice:

1 *From the desktop, double click on the 'Start' icon and click on 'Documents'. As an alternative you can click on the small yellow folder in the Taskbar at the bottom of the screen. This will take you to the last folder you had open or will show you the four libraries mentioned above.*
2 *This will open a new window that will show you all of the work that is stored in this folder.*

If it's a brand new computer, there will be nothing in it.

3 *Click on the 'Start' icon in the bottom left-hand corner and open Word again.*

You have now got two things open: Documents and Word. You are now multi-tasking! To switch between the two things that are open, you just click on them in the Taskbar at the bottom of the screen as described previously. Try this now.

There is another way of switching between windows in Windows 7 called Aero Flip 3D. This lets you see 3D images of all of the windows that you have open. You can then scroll through them and select the one you want to work on. To do this:

1 *Hold down CTRL and the Windows logo key. Now press the TAB key. The screen will now look something like this:*

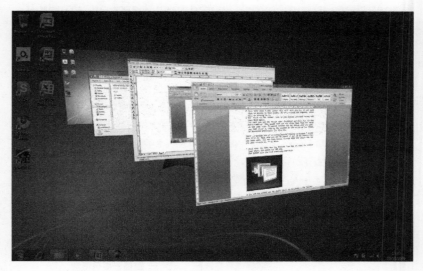

2 *You can now either use the scroll wheel on your mouse or the TAB key on your keyboard to scroll through all of the open windows. When you get to the one you want to work with, click the mouse on it or press ENTER. This window will then be shown full screen.*

3 *Click on 'Documents' in the Taskbar and then click on the cross in the top right-hand corner of the window to close it.*

Word will still be open. Leave it open for now, as we will use it to look at some of the standard features of software.

If you ever want to get back to your desktop quickly you do not have to close or minimize all the open windows.

1 *Move the mouse into the very right-hand bottom of the screen where you can see a small rectangle:*

2 *Hold the mouse over the rectangle and it will make any windows that are open transparent so you can see the desktop beneath.*

3 *Click on the rectangle and you are taken directly to the desktop.*

4 *Click on the rectangle again to go back to the last window that you were working on.*

4.7 Internet Explorer basics

In this book will be visiting lots of different websites. You will be using Internet Explorer to find and view all of these sites. Internet Explorer 8 is shown below. From here you can access the millions of pages of information that exist across the world.

Most of the screen is used to display the contents of the website (Google in this case). Notice at the top of the screen, what is called the address bar. All websites have a unique address, and this is where you can type in that address (if you know) it and Internet Explorer will then display that website. The address shown here is for the Google website.

For example, to get to the BBC website:

1 *Click in the address bar. Notice the little line flashing. This is the cursor and it shows you where you have clicked on the screen. When you start typing the text will appear wherever the cursor is.*

2 *Type www.bbc.co.uk into the address bar and press ENTER. The BBC website is now displayed.*

3 *If you find that the text is too small, you can click on the little magnifying glass in the bottom left-hand corner until the text size is suitable for you.*

4 *Now close down Internet Explorer by clicking on the cross in the top right-hand corner.*

Hints and tips

The terms 'websites' and 'sites' are used interchangeably because they mean exactly the same thing.

4.8 Switching off the computer

You might not want to do this just yet, but it is worth having a practice now. Remember that you don't actually press the on/off button to switch the computer off – that would be far too easy. Instead you do the following:

1 *Click on the 'Start' icon in the bottom left-hand corner.*

2 *Click on 'Shut Down' from the options listed.*
3 *Click 'OK'.*

Your computer may take a while to switch itself off, but after a few seconds it will shut itself down. Note that you can access other options for shutting down by clicking on the small arrow to the right of the 'Shut down' option. For example, you can put your computer into 'Sleep' mode if you are planning to use it again soon. This reduces the time it takes to get up and running when you switch it back on again.

Hints and tips

It is important that you shut down the computer using this method. It carries out various checks as it shuts down to make sure that it is done properly. Switching off using the on/off switch will cause problems when you come to switch on again. You should only use the on/off switch when the normal shut down routine won't work – this sometimes happens.

When the computer shuts down it should also turn off the monitor, so you probably do not need to switch this off separately.

IMPORTANT THINGS TO REMEMBER FROM THIS CHAPTER

1 *When you switch the computer on it will go through a routine that may take a few minutes. This is setting up the computer so that it works properly.*

2 *You use the mouse to move a pointer on the screen and then click on images to make things happen.*

3 *Your mouse has a left and right button. Different things happen depending on where you click and which button you use.*

4 *Your mouse may also have a scroll wheel that allows you to move the pointer up and down on the screen.*

5 *On your computer keyboard, in addition to the letters of the alphabet there are other keys, such as ENTER which have special functions.*

6 *You can open programs by clicking on small images called icons. Each program has its own icon so you can tell which is which.*

7 *Folders are locations on the computer where information is stored. For example, there is a folder for documents.*

8 *All programs and folders open in windows. You can have lots of open at the same time and flip between them in a number of ways.*

9 *Internet Explorer is the software that you use to get onto the Internet. You can type the address of the website into the address bar.*

10 *You need to switch off the computer via the Start menu so that it can close down properly. You should never switch it off using the on/off switch!*

5

Setting up your email address

In this chapter you will learn
- *the basics of email*
- *the difference between standard email and web-based email*
- *whether to use standard or web-based email*
- *how to set up web-based email software*
- *how to set up Microsoft Outlook*

5.1 Email software

There are two main types of email software. The first is standard **email software** such as Microsoft Outlook, which comes as part of some versions of the Microsoft Office package. As an alternative you can use Windows Live Mail, which is available as a free download. If you do have Outlook this will already be installed and set up on your computer and you run it from your desktop in the same way as other programs. If you have had a new computer set up by your supplier, this may have been set up for you. If not, then section 5.5 of this chapter will show you how to do it.

Hints and tips

If you are buying a new computer you should ask the shop if they would set an ISP and an email address up for you. It can be quite tricky to do at this early stage of your computing career!

The second type is what is called **web-based** email. With this, you do not need to have email software installed your computer, as you can get access to it using the Internet. Web-based email is generally free. For example, Microsoft Hotmail, Google's Gmail and YahooMail are all free-to-use web-based email services. You may also be given free email addresses from your Internet Service Provider (the company you get your Internet connection from). For example, BT, AOL and Tiscali all provide free web-based email too.

All email software has the same basic functions whether you use a standard or web-based one. Whichever one you choose, you will need to know your email address (i.e. if the shop have set one up for you) or create an email address if you are setting up for yourself.

Hints and tips

There are so many different email providers that it can be difficult to know which to choose. Some people have several different email addresses that they use for different things. When you are starting out, it's best to choose one email address and stick with it.

5.2 Email basics

Email stands for electronic mail and the easiest way to think of it is as an electronic letter. You do not have to print it out and send it – instead, it is sent electronically over the Internet. Therefore, you must have Internet access in order to use email.

Like normal mail, emails are sent and received using addresses. All email addresses follow the same format. For example: marjorie.franklin@googlemail.com. The bit before the @ sign is usually used to identify the individual, and the bit after is the name of the **email provider**.

Hints and tips

Email has been around for many years now and has millions of users. Therefore you might not get the email address you want, as there is probably already someone out there with the same name as you who has already bagged the address.

5.3 Choosing which email software to use

Choosing which email provider to use can be quite difficult. There is a lot of debate over which is the 'best'. Much of it depends on your personal preferences and the way in which you want to access your emails. It also depends on what software is already on your computer and whether you are prepared to pay for new software if you don't have it already. Most individual users tend to go for a free web-based email.

Hints and tips

If in doubt, go for a web-based email as these are easier to set up. In this book we will be looking at Gmail, which is a free email service provided by Google.

Reasons to choose web-based email

▶ *You can access your email from any computer. Therefore, if you don't have your own computer, or are away from home and want to access your emails perhaps from a library or Internet cafe, then this is the choice for you.*

▶ *If you do not already have email software on your computer and you don't want to buy or download any, then it is simpler to set up and use a web-based email service.*

▶ *It's completely free and you can have several different addresses if you want to.*

▶ *You get access to other websites. For example, if you get a Gmail account with Google, you can then use their* **chat rooms** *and* **blogging** *websites without having to register again.*

Reasons to choose standard email

▶ *You may already have the email software on your computer, and it may already have been set up for you when you bought it. If this is the case, this will save you the time of setting up a web-based email.*

▶ *Web-based emails can be cut off if you don't use them for a while. Most web-based emails will be cut*

*off after a month if you have not sent or received an
email in that time.*

▶ *If your connection to the Internet is not available
for any reason, you cannot get at old messages with
web-based mail, but you can with standard email.*

▶ *It is claimed that it is more secure as your emails
are stored on your computer rather than on the
Internet. See Chapter 15 for more advice on keeping
your information secure.*

5.4 Setting up a web-based email address

In this example, we will be using Gmail, which is a free
email service provided by Google.

1 *Open Internet Explorer, by clicking on the icon in
the Taskbar, or by clicking on 'Start' and clicking
on it from the list.*

2 *In the address bar, type www.gmail.com as shown:*

3 *Press ENTER or you can click the blue arrow to the
right of the address bar. The Gmail web page will
now be displayed in the main window:*

4 *Many services are provided free on the Internet, but
the websites offering them, usually make you register
with them first. This involves filling in an* **online
form.** *You will get familiar with this process as you*

use the Internet more, although it might take a while the first time you do it. Move the mouse over the text that reads 'Create an account'. Notice that the pointer changes to a hand with one finger pointing. 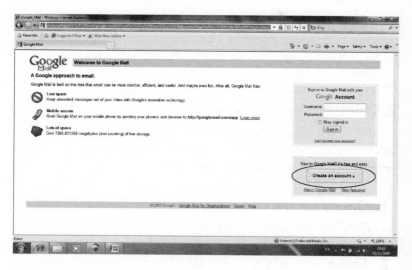 *This pointer image means that you are on a* **hyperlink** *or* **link**. *This will take you to another page.*

5 *Click on the text 'Create an account'. You will now be asked to fill in the form.*

6 *Click in the box where an answer is needed, e.g. First Name.*

7 *Type in your answer. Use the SHIFT key if you want letters in capitals.*

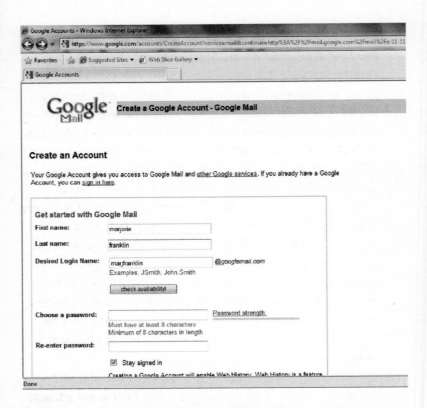

8 *Carry on doing this for all of the boxes, filling in the information that is asked for. You can tell which box you are in by looking for the cursor (the small vertical flashing line). If you do anything wrong it will ask you to fill in the box again. In this example, we have set it up for someone called Marjorie Franklin, but you will need to choose the name that you want to use.*

Email addresses

Your email address does not have to be your real name. Remember that you will be giving

this address to people so they can email you.
Bunnykins@gmail.com might not be appropriate
if you are going to be emailing the vicar!

9 *After you have typed in your desired email address,
click the 'Check availability' button. This will tell you
whether someone else has already got that address.
If your name is John Smith, then you're in trouble!*

10 *You are now asked for a password. Passwords
mean that only you can log on to this email address,
so they are very important. Choose one that you
will remember. It also has to be a good password,
which means that you have letters and numbers in
it. (This makes them harder for people to guess.)
Some websites require passwords to have a certain
number of characters to make them more secure.*

11 *You have to type the password again in the box
underneath.*

12 *You need to move down the page to fill the rest
of the form in. Use the scroll wheel on your mouse
(if it has one) or click several times on the arrow
at the bottom of the scroll bar on the right of the
screen. This is called* **scrolling**.

13 *You need to complete the Security Question and
Answer box. But you can leave the Secondary email
box empty. The idea of the security question is that
if you forget your password, you can get a reminder
by entering this information.*

14 *Type the words shown in Word verification box.
This is a security measure to ensure that only
humans and not hackers' programs are creating the
email account. In this case the word is 'cordneria'
but it will be something different on yours.*

15 *Scroll down to the bottom of the page and click the 'I accept. Create my account' button. You should see a screen, which tells you that you have successfully set up your Gmail account.*

16 *You will be asked to verify your account, which is sometimes done by sending you a text to your mobile phone. This should be instant and you will be prompted to type in the code that you have received.*

> You have to type your email address and password in every time you want to check your email so it is important that you remember them, or you will have to set them up all over again.

Congratulations – you have now set up your email.

1 *Click on 'I'm ready – show me my account' and you are ready to send and receive emails.*

2 *When you want to access your emails all you need to do is open Internet Explorer, go to the www.gmail.com website and type in your user name and password. You can do this on any computer that is connected to the Internet.*

5.5 Setting up Microsoft Outlook

If you don't have Microsoft Outlook you can skip this section. The instructions here show you how to set up Microsoft Outlook to use with the Gmail address although it is possible to use other addresses.

In this example we will use Gmail as our email provider, and will set it up so that we can use the Gmail address through Microsoft Outlook.

1 *Double click on Microsoft Outlook on the desktop, or go to the 'Start' menu and 'All programs' and click on it from the list. If you can't find it, it probably means that you haven't got it on your computer so you will either have to buy it and install it, or use a web-based email as described earlier.*

2 *Assuming this is the first time you have used Microsoft Office it will work through a series of screens prompting you for information that you need to set it up. This is called a '**wizard**'.*

3 *Click on 'Next'.*

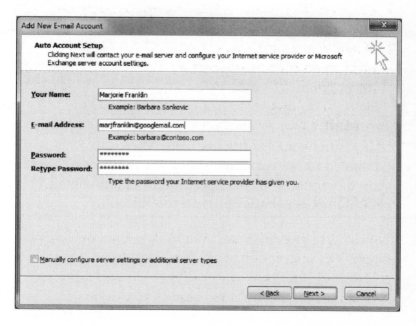

4 *Type in the email address you have just set up and the name that you want to appear on your emails when you send them to people, and click 'Next'.*

Outlook will now take a few seconds to configure itself and will then open up your email ready to use. The screen will look something like this:

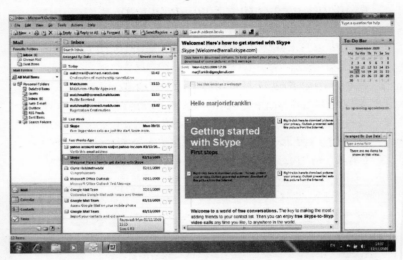

Live Mail

This is free email software, from Microsoft, designed to be used with Windows computers. You can download it from download.live.com/wlmail. Setting up is a similar process to Outlook.

IMPORTANT THINGS TO REMEMBER FROM THIS CHAPTER

1 There are two main ways of using email. You can use standard email that is installed on your PC or go to the websites of email providers.

2 Microsoft Outlook is an example of standard email software. Alternatively you can use web-based services that are provided by websites such as Hotmail, AOL, Tiscali and BT.

3 All email has the same standard features, for example to send, and receive emails, handle attachments and use contacts lists.

4 If you learn how to use one type of email you should find it quite easy to use a different email later on as they are all very similar.

5 There are merits to both standard or web-based email so you decide about which is most suitable for you. If in doubt, it is probably best to go for a web-based email.

6 You need to create an email address by registering with an email provider. Your email address will be unique to you.

7 Email addresses are made up of a name that identifies you and the name of the email provider e.g. marjfranklin@googlemail.com.

8 The registration process may take some time if it is the first time you have used the Internet.

9 You can have numerous email addresses as most email is free. However, it is probably best to choose one and stick with it.

10 You can set up Microsoft Outlook to work with web-based email if you want to.

6

··

Sending and receiving emails

In this chapter you will learn
- *how to open your email software*
- *how to look at messages that you have received*
- *how to send a message*
- *how to read and reply to messages*

6.1 Introduction

If you do not already have an **email address**, you will
need to go back to Chapter 5, which shows you how to
set one up. As you may have seen, there are lots of email
providers to choose from and each one is slightly different.
However, they all share some common characteristics.

This chapter will use Gmail (also known as Googlemail)
as an example. At the time this book was written, this
was one of the most widely used email programs. If
you are using another type of email such as Outlook,
Yahoo, or Tiscali for example, then your screens will
look different to those shown here. However, the basic
principles remain the same whichever email you are using.

6.2 The basic functions of email

To start with, we will have a look at the standard features of email and what they do.

1 *Open Internet Explorer and type www.gmail.com into the address bar.*

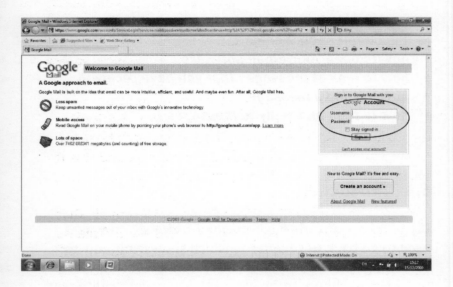

2 *Type in your email address and password on the right-hand side.*
3 *The main email page will now open. Most of what you do can be done from here. We have labelled two of the main areas.*

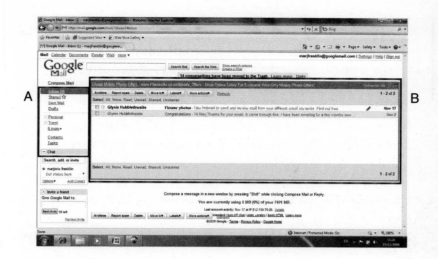

Area A: From here you can create new emails by clicking on the 'Compose Mail' link or you can look through the folders where emails are stored. The main folder you will be using is called your Inbox and this is where any emails you receive will go.

Area B: This part of the page lists all of the emails that are in whichever folder you have clicked on in Area A. The standard setting is for it to display the contents of your Inbox.

Notice that unread messages are usually in bold so that you spot them. Also, next to Inbox in Area A there is a number in brackets which indicated how many emails you have that you haven't yet read.

Hints and tips

You will need to know the email address of someone else so that you can practise sending and receiving emails with them.

There will already be at least one message in your Inbox from Google Mail welcoming you to the software.

1 *To view an email, click on it in Area B. Area B will now change showing the content on the email.*

2 *Once you have read the message there are a number of things you can do with it such as reply to it, or delete it. We will come back to these later.*

6.3 Sending an email

1 *Click on 'Compose Mail' in the top left-hand corner. Note that Area B has changed again. This time it is ready for you to send an email.*

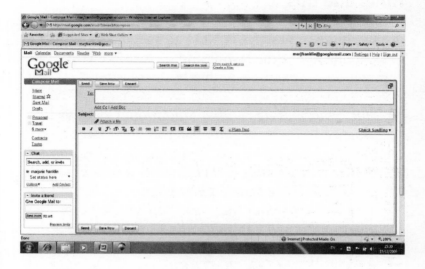

2 *You need to know the email address of the person that you want to send this email to. Type the email address into the box next to where it says To: It is important that you get the address exactly right or your message will not be sent.*

3 *The 'Add cc' option can be used to send the same email to someone else. If you want to do this, click on 'Add cc' and type the email address of the second person.*

4 *In the Subject: box, type a heading for what your email is about.*

5 *Click in the big white box. This is where you will type in your message. Think of this white space as a piece of paper on to which you are writing (typing) the message that you want to send. It can be as short or long as you like.*

Hints and tips

Emails among friends are usually quite informal and common practice is NOT to spend ages worrying about the layout and format like you might do for example with a business letter.

6 *Start your message with a salutation. Common practice seems to be 'Hi', but you don't have to do that. So type 'Hi Glynis' and press ENTER twice. Notice that pressing ENTER starts a new line, so pressing it twice leaves a blank line.*

7 *You now type your message. You can just type away and it will automatically start on a new line when it needs to. If you want to start a new paragraph just press ENTER twice. Notice that lines have been left between the paragraphs in this case. Also notice the standard use of capital letters, which is achieved by holding down the SHIFT key as you type the letter that you want to be a capital.*

8 *Common practice is to put your name at the bottom of the email, perhaps with an informal sign off such as 'Regards' or 'Cheers' but there are no hard and fast rules.*

9 *Click 'Send' in the bottom left-hand corner of this window.*

That's it. Your message now flies across cyberspace and will appear in the inbox of the person you sent it to. In most cases, this will be almost instant, but sometimes it may take a few minutes or even hours for the message to be received.

Correcting errors

If you make a mistake when typing use the DELETE key or the BACKSPACE key to delete the error and then re-type.

For example, to change 'Glynes' to 'Glynis' as it should be:

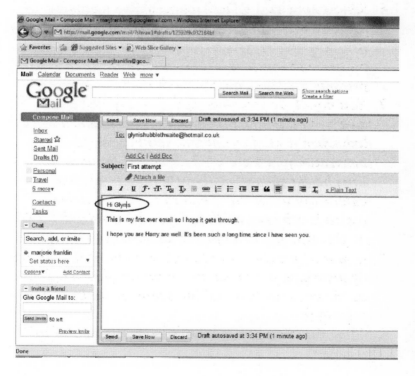

1 *Move the mouse to just before or just after the error and click. There is a small line called the* **cursor,** *which shows you where you are. If you start typing now it will put the text where the cursor is.*
2 *Delete the letter 'e' by pressing the BACKSPACE key and then type the letter 'i'. Note that BACKSPACE deletes the character to the left of the cursor and the DELETE key deletes the character to the right.*

If you want to delete lots of text, you keep pressing BACKSPACE or DELETE. An alternative method is to **highlight** the text you want to delete and delete it all in one go.

For example, to delete the whole of the first sentence:

1 *Point the mouse just before the T of 'This' on the first line, then hold down the left button. Move the mouse to just after the exclamation mark. You will see that all of the text in-between is now highlighted.*
2 *Let go of the left mouse button and press the DELETE key. The whole block of text is gone.*

Hints and tips

You can use this highlighting technique in any program. It may take a while to getting used to holding the button down and moving the mouse at the same time.

6.4 Saving your email

When you send an email a copy of it will be stored automatically in the 'Sent Items' folder. If you want to go back to an email you have sent previously, you can click on 'Sent Mail', find the email in the list and double click on it to read it.

You might also find it useful to save your email as you go along. For example, if you were typing quite a long email and then something went wrong or you deleted it by accident, you would have to start typing all over again. What you can do is save a 'draft' version of the email so that if this did happen you can go back to the saved draft. To do this:

1 *You can save your message at any time when you are typing it by clicking on 'Save Now' from the menu options at the top of Area B. You will see a message telling you that a copy of the email has been saved into the 'Drafts' folder.*
2 *If you need to get back to the draft version, click on the 'Drafts' folder and then double click on the message. The message will then be on the screen and you can carry on typing, or send the message.*

6.5 Receiving and replying to emails

When people send you an email it will appear in your Inbox. You have already seen this in Section 6.2 when you opened the welcome email from the Gmail team. All the messages received go into your Inbox and are stored there whether you have read them or not. When you load your email it will show you how many new emails you have got. You can then open up your Inbox and read them. If you are using email for the first time, you might have to wait for your friends to reply to the one you have just sent, or you could find someone who you know uses email, give them your new email address and ask them to email you so you can check it all works okay.

In this example, Marjorie has got an email back from her friend Glynis. To read and then reply to an email:

1 *Click on the message so that it is* **highlighted** *as shown. The message itself will now open.*

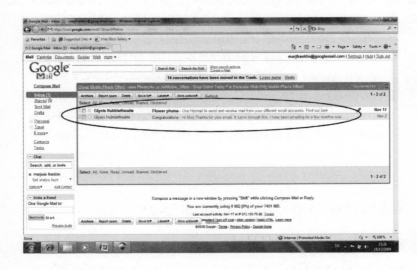

2 *To reply to this message, click on 'Reply' from the options.*

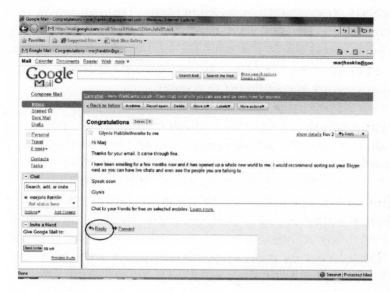

3 *A new window will open showing the original message.*

4 *Replying to a message is almost the same as sending on as described in section 6.3. It is actually slightly easier because you will see that it has put their email address in automatically so you don't need to remember it.*

5 *Type your reply and click on 'Send'.*

6.6 Printing and deleting emails

Every time you go into Gmail from now on you will need to check your Inbox to see if you have got any new messages. You can then read them and reply to them if you want to. All emails will just sit in your Inbox forever until you delete them. You can delete messages after you have read them, or you can keep them if you think you need to. You might want to print an email out, either to keep as a record, or if you need a paper copy for some other reason.

Some email you get will be junk email (called **spam**) and you should just delete it without even reading it. Some email software has a separate folder called 'Spam' where it automatically puts emails if it thinks they are junk email. As a general rule, you should never open an email unless you recognize who it is from – you should just delete it. Sometimes real emails can get put into the Spam folder by mistake so it is always worth checking to see if you recognize the email address before you delete them.

To delete an email from your Inbox:

1 *Click on the Inbox so that all messages are shown. Note that as you receive more messages your Inbox will fill up and you may need to scroll down to see them all. Some email systems will divide the message headers between several pages, displaying only a certain number on each. This can get very confusing after a while so it is a good idea to delete emails that you no longer need.*
2 *Click on the message that you want to delete.*

3 *Select 'delete' from the options at the top of the window where the message is displayed.*

To print an email:

1 *Click on the email you want to print, in the Inbox. It will then open in a new window.*
2 *Click on the 'Print' icon.*

IMPORTANT THINGS TO REMEMBER FROM THIS CHAPTER

1   *Gmail or Google Mail is just one of many email providers. They are all very similar in terms of the features they offer.*

2   *The first thing you have to do is log onto the email provider's website using the email address and password that you have set up.*

3   *The main feature of any email system is the ability to compose and send messages. To do this you need to know the email address of the person to sent it to.*

4   *The Inbox is the main folder into which all incoming emails will be stored. Emails stay in the Inbox until you delete them.*

5   *Emails you have not yet read are normally at the top of the list and are usually shown in bold.*

6   *There are some informal rules as to how to write emails although you don't have to stick to these. Emails between friends may be very informal.*

7   *You can save copies of email that you have sent. This is useful if you want to keep a record of what you sent.*

8 When you receive an email you can read it and then reply to it without having to know the email address of the person you are sending it to.

9 You can print copies of emails if you want a paper copy.

10 It is good practice to delete emails this regularly or your Inbox can become full.

7

Sending and receiving email attachments

In this chapter you will learn
- *what an attachment is*
- *what can be attached and sent using email*
- *how to find what you want to attach*
- *how to send an attachment*
- *how to receive an attachment*

7.1 Introduction

When you send an email, you are sending some text from one computer to another. If you want to send other things too, you can do this using an **attachment**. Everything that is on your computer whether it is a document, a photograph, a piece of music, or a video clip, is stored in a **file**. In turn these files are stored in **libraries** and **folders**. To send an attachment, you are basically attaching one of these files to your email and it will be sent at the same time as the text message.

This does present a small problem in that you need to know which file contains the information you want to send, and which library and folder it is stored in. For example, if you had a photograph that you wanted to send to someone, you would have to know the name of the file that contains the photograph, and the name of the folder that the file is stored in.

Hints and tips

Think of your computer as a giant filing cabinet full of folders and files. Like a real filing cabinet you need to know where everything is filed if you ever want to find it again.

7.2 Understanding libraries, folders and files

We had a quick look at folders in Chapter 4. It is worth explaining them in a little more detail here as when you send or receive an attachment you have to send it from, or receive it into a folder. There are lots of folders on your computer already, and you can create your own if you want to. Folders are usually stored in one of four main libraries called Documents, Music, Pictures and Videos. When you first start using a new computer, it will have these four libraries. You will add folders to these to store different files, or you can store files straight into the library.

1 *To open the 'Documents' library, click on the Start button and select 'Documents'.*

The 'Documents' library will be slightly different on every computer you use, so yours may not look exactly the same as this.

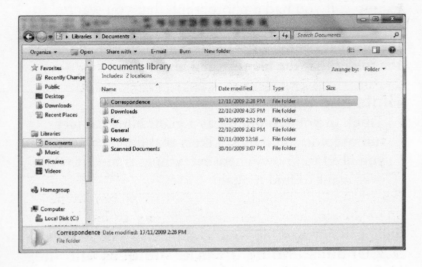

In this example there are some folders shown with the small yellow icon shaped like a folder.

   2 *To find out what is in a folder, double click on it.*
   3 *To view a different library, e.g. Pictures, click on it on the left-hand side.*

In this example, the 'Pictures' library has been clicked on. Inside it there is a folder called 'Sample Pictures' and several photos.

   4 *To see what is inside a folder, double click on it.*

For example, within the Music library there may be
an **iTunes** folder containing lots of music files. You
will probably be using your computer for other things
as well, such as writing letters, or storing digital
photographs. If this is the case, you will have come
across the libraries, because every time you save
anything, you are asked which library you want to
save into.

5 *Click on the cross to close this down.*

We will now look at how you use email to send and
receive one of the photos. The same process applies to
files that you want to send via email.

It would be useful if you could find a file, perhaps a
photograph that you can send to someone as a test.

7.3 Sending an attachment

1 *Open Google Mail if it is not already open by opening Internet Explorer and typing www.gmail. com into the address bar. You will need to log in with your email address and password.*
2 *Click on 'Compose Mail' in the top left-hand corner.*
3 *You can now write your email as described in the previous chapter, adding the email address of the person you are writing to, and filling in the subject line, and then typing your message.*
4 *To add an attachment, click on 'Attach a File'.*

Windows Explorer will now open. Yours may not look exactly the same as this.

This is where you need to know the name of the library, folder and the file that you want to attach. If it is a photograph, it is most likely that it will be in the 'Pictures library'. If it is music, it is likely to be in the 'Music library'. Other types of files usually get saved into the 'Documents' library. You may have set up some of your own folders within each of these libraries.

5 *For this example, double click on 'Libraries' and then double click on 'Pictures'.*
6 *Click on the file that you want to send. If you want to send more than one, then hold the CTRL key down and then click on each one you want to send.*

7 *Click on 'Open'. In this example we have attached two photos. You can see that they are attached as their file names are shown.*

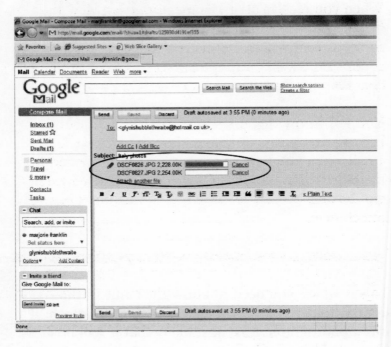

8 *Finish off the main text of your email and when you are ready, click 'Send' and the photos will be sent with the email.*

Hints and tips

Some files may take a while to send, especially photograph or music files.

7.4 Receiving an attachment

When you receive an attachment you can view the file and save it onto your computer. For example, if someone sent you a photograph as an attachment, you could view the photograph and then save it onto your computer so you have got your own copy of it.

You will know that an email has an attachment, because you will see a paper clip symbol next to the email when you look in your Inbox. In this example, the paper clip is very small but you can see where it will be displayed. The last email in the Inbox has an attachment.

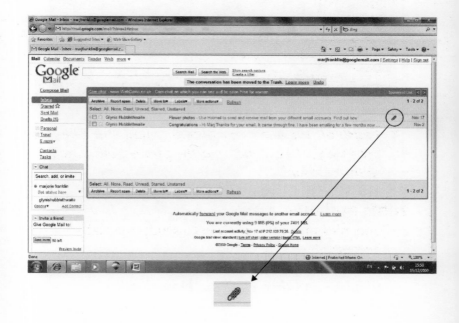

1 *Move the mouse to the message and click on it.*
2 *The message will now open in its own window and you can see the name of the file that has been attached. In this case there are two called 'Flowers 1.jpg' and 'Flowers 2.jpg'. You can see a small version of the image within the email.*
3 *To open the attachment, click on it. It will then open. As this is a picture, it will open up and let you see the picture.*

4 *To save the picture onto your computer, close this window and then click on 'Download'.*

5 *You are prompted to save it into a particular folder. Select the 'Pictures' library on the left-hand side as shown and click on 'Save'.*

6 *Go back to your email and reply to it, or delete it. You can safely delete the message now because you have saved the attachment onto your own computer. If you deleted the message without saving the attachment first, you would delete the attachment too.*

7 *You can view the photograph at any time without having to use email. Click on the Start button then on 'Pictures'.*

8 *Find the 'Flowers1.jpg' file and double click on it. It will then open for you to view.*

IMPORTANT THINGS TO REMEMBER FROM THIS CHAPTER

1 An attachment is a way of sending a file to someone via email. Files can contain all kinds of information, for example documents or photographs.

2 You need to know which file you want to send and where it is stored on your computer.

3 Your computer stores files inside four main libraries • called Documents, Music, Videos and Pictures. Within each library you can set up folders to help organize your work.

4 At this stage it is easiest to use the four libraries that are already set up. For example, store photographs in the Pictures library.

5 When viewing the content of libraries and folders, Windows will show you thumbnail views (small images) of the files.

6 To send an attachment, use the 'Attach a File' option when sending an email and then send it in the normal way.

7 If you receive an email with an attachment you can download it onto your own computer so that you have your own copy of it.

8 *Once you have downloaded a file you can access it from your computer without having to go back onto your email.*

9 *Windows will open attachments using appropriate software. For example, if the attachment is a photograph, it will use its own viewer to show you the image.*

10 *Photographs may also be displayed within the body of the email.*

Organizing email messages and contacts

In this chapter you will learn
- *how to manage folders in email*
- *how to add and remove contacts from your address book*
- *how to send emails to your contacts*

8.1 Introduction

Even if you only use email occasionally, it is worth being organized. Every time you send and receive an email, a copy of the email is stored in folders within the email software. After a while these folders can get full which can make it hard to find old messages if you need to, and it can make email run slower.

Also you will be using email addresses. All email software has a facility for storing your contacts' details. This is sometimes called an address book and in that you can store people's names and email addresses.

This chapter will show you how to keep track of the folders and how to manage your **contacts**.

8.2 Organizing the folders

In the last chapter we looked at the way that your computer has **folders** that it uses to store **files**. Email works in a similar way in that it has folders, which it uses to store emails. Let's look at the folders now.

1 *Open Google Mail. The folders are listed on the left-hand side.*

The basic set-up for the folders is that every message you ever receive is stored in a folder called the Inbox. You have already used the Inbox to read messages. The messages will stay there until you delete them. Also, every message you ever send is stored in the folder called Sent Mail. Again, these will stay there until you delete them.

Another useful folder is the Drafts folder. If you save any part-written emails they go in here. Also Google Mail will do an auto-save if you have been typing for a while.

Also notice that there is a link to '6 more' folders. Useful ones in here are the Spam and Trash folders. Spam is where junk emails go automatically but sometimes some genuine ones end up in here. Trash is where emails go after you have deleted them. Eventually they will disappear from here but you they are still here for a while in case you delete one by accident.

You can access any one of these folders in the same way as the Inbox folder by clicking on it. The contents of the folder are then shown.

Creating folders

In addition to these standard folders you can create your own. But I suggest that you only do this if you use email a lot for different reasons and need to be keep messages separately, or if you are one of those really organized people!

▶ To create a new folder, click on the 'New label' option and type in a suitable name for this folder. This will then be displayed with the other folders in the left-hand side.

Moving messages

All new emails will automatically go into your Inbox. You may want to move messages out of your Inbox into a new folder. To do this:

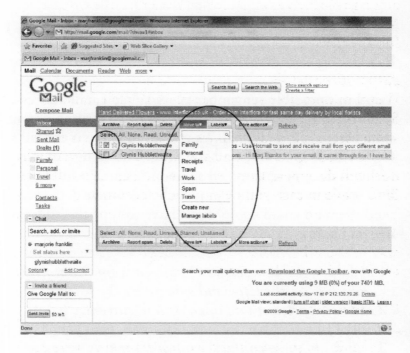

1 Click in the small box to the left of the message. When you do this a 'tick' will appear. You can tick as many messages as you like here.

2 Click 'Move to' and all of your folders are shown.

3 *Click on the folder that you want to move it to, and click 'OK'. The message has now been moved.*

You can do other things from this menu using the same method of ticking the messages. One particularly useful feature is that you can tick all the messages that you no longer want and then click on 'Delete' to get rid of lots of un-needed messages all in one go.

8.3 Using the contacts list

You can't possibly remember every single email address that you will ever use and having them all written down somewhere is impractical. That's why there is a contacts facility built in to all email software. The beauty of this is that once you have typed someone's email address into your contacts, you can just click on their details to send them an email – you don't have to type the address in ever again.

1 *To open the contacts in Gmail, click on 'Contacts' which is on the left-hand side under the folders.*
2 *The contacts list will open. It will currently be empty as we have not put any contacts in yet.*
3 *Click on 'New contact' icon as shown. A screen will be displayed into which you can type all the contact details for one person.*

4 *You don't have to fill all of this in but you will probably want to type in their name and email address.*

5 *Click on 'Save' when you have finished.*

6 *Repeat this process every time you want to add a new contact.*

7 *To change any of the details, you double click on the person and then click on 'Name' and you get back to the same screen to make changes.*

8 *Click on the cross to close the contacts.*

9 *Click on 'Mail' in the bottom left-hand corner to get back to your Inbox.*

10 *To send an email to someone in your contacts, click on 'Compose Mail' in the usual way.*

11 *Click on 'To:'. This will open the contacts list.*

12 *Click once on the address of the person you want to send the email to. Then click on 'Done'.*

13 *Finish and send your email in the usual way.*

In this example there is only one person in the contacts list but you are likely to have lots of people in yours. If you want to send the same message to lots of people, then repeat step 11 for all the people you want to receive the email.

Hints and tips

The 'Add cc' link indicates 'copy to' which means that you are sending them a copy for information although they are not the main recipient. The main recipient will know that this other person has also got the email. The 'Add bcc' link is a blind copy, which means you can send someone else a copy of the email and the main recipient won't know that this person is also getting a copy.

IMPORTANT THINGS TO REMEMBER FROM THIS CHAPTER

1 *Even if you only use email occasionally it is worth getting organized.*

2 *Emails are stored in folders. The Inbox is the folder where all email is delivered to.*

3 *Other common folders include 'Drafts' where you can save a copy of emails that you are working on.*

4 *'Sent Mail' holds copies of every email you send.*

5 *'Trash' is where emails go after you have deleted them. If you deleted them by mistake, move them from here to another folder.*

6 *You can create your own folders to store emails. For example, you might set one up for work or family emails.*

7 *You can delete emails or move them into suitable folders to keep your Inbox tidy.*

8 *The contacts list is like an online address book where you can store people's email addresses.*

9 *You can also store a range of other personal details of people in the contacts list.*

10 *Contacts lists save time and effort as you don't have to remember everyone's email address as you can simply click on it from a list.*

9

Getting started on the Internet

In this chapter you will learn
- *what the Internet is*
- *how to type in a 'web address'*
- *what a hyperlink is and how to follow one*
- *how to move forward and back through web pages*
- *how to use a 'search engine'*
- *how to assess whether a website is reliable*
- *what to do when websites don't work*

9.1 Introduction

The Internet is a worldwide connection of computers. It can be used for communicating and sharing information in many ways, and the most important of these is the **World Wide Web (www)**. This is made up of millions and millions of pages of information, and the links between them. These pages are called **web pages**. A collection of web pages is called a **website**. All sorts of organizations and individuals might create a website. In many cases these are businesses trying to sell things, but also include government organizations, charities, clubs and private individuals.

This presents a few problems. The first is that there is so much information available that it can be difficult to find what you need. The second is that there is an awful lot of rubbish in among the good stuff. The third is that the information on the Web is constantly changing. New websites are being put up all the time, websites are being removed and also the content of individual websites is constantly changing.

Hints and tips

The Internet or Net refers to the global connection of computers. The World Wide Web or Web refers to some of the information that is available on the Internet.

9.2 Finding a website when you know the web address

The easiest way to find a website is if you know the **address**. Website addresses are unique, so no two websites can have exactly the same name. Most organizations advertise their web addresses and include them in their advertising. For example: www.oxfam.org.uk.

Tips and hints

Internet Explorer is what is known as a web **browser** – a program that displays the contents of websites and handles the links between them. Internet Explorer is the most widely used but there are other web browsers available such as Mozilla, Netscape and Google Chrome. These work in exactly the same way, but look slightly different.

To go to a website if you know the address:

1 *Double click on the Internet Explorer icon on the desktop or click on the icon in the Taskbar.*

Internet Explorer will now load and a web page will be displayed. The first page to be shown is known as your **home page***. In this case, the home page is Tiscali, which is an ISP. Yours might be something completely different.*

Circled at the top of the window is the **address bar**. This is where it shows the address of the page you are on, and where you type the address of the page that you want to go to.

2 *Click in the address bar and type in the address of the website you want to go to, in this case* www.oxfam.org.uk*. It is very important that you type the address exactly as shown with the correct slashes and full stops where relevant.*

3 *Press ENTER or click on the green arrow to the right of the address bar.*

After a few seconds, you will be taken to the page with the address that you have just typed in.

When you get to the page, it is probably the 'home page' of the website. This time 'home page' refers to the main page of a website. It will usually contain general information that welcomes you to the site and tells you about the organization or person who is responsible for it.

Once you are in the website, you may need to move to other parts of the website to find what you want. Nearly all web pages include links to other pages. These links are called **hyperlinks**. They might take you to another page on the same website, or to a page on another website.

Hyperlinks can be attached to anything. There might be a link from a piece of text, or from a picture. They try to make it easy for you to spot the links and explain where the link will take you. The **mouse pointer**, which normally looks like this ▷ will change when you hover the mouse over an object on a web page. If it changes to a little hand like this 🖑 that means that there is a link to another page.

4 *Find a hyperlink (any hyperlink) and click on it. It will probably take you to a different web page, and this may have lots of information on it, and more hyperlinks.*

5 *You can quite quickly lose track of where you are. After you have clicked on a few hyperlinks, you have lost the page where you started. If this happens and you want to return to it, click the 'Back' button, which is the arrow (pointing left) in the top left-hand corner of the window. This will take you to the previous page.*

6 *Click the 'Back' button again. This will take you back to the page before that, and so on until eventually you are back where you started.*

Hints and tips

The 'Back' button will only work if you have already been to some web pages. Otherwise there will be nothing for it to go back to. If the arrow is in a blue circle it means that there are pages to go back to. If it is in a grey circle, then there are no pages to go back to.

Another problem is that sometimes when you click on a hyperlink, a new window opens up. This means that your original page is still open in the background. To get back to the original page in this case:

▶ *Click on the small cross in the top right-hand corner of the window. This window then closes, and your original page is displayed again.*

9.3 Structure of web addresses

It is useful to be able to recognize the way that web addresses are put together. Sometimes it will give you a hint about the nature of the site. Most addresses look like this: www.hodder.co.uk.

▶ *The www means World Wide Web and most (but not all) addresses start with this. In most cases you don't even need to type this in.*

- ▶ *The next part tells you the name of the individual or organization who owns the website. In this case it is <u>hodder</u> (the publisher of this book).*
- ▶ *The last part of the address tells you what type of organization or person owns the website and where it is in the world. The table below shows some common examples.*

.com	*Stands for 'commercial' and will be a business. Could be anywhere in the world.*
.co.uk	*a UK business.*
.org.uk	*a UK organization, but not a business, e.g. a charity.*
.gov.uk	*a UK government website.*
.ac.uk	*a UK college or university. The 'ac' is short for academic.*
au, it, de	*These are country codes that appear at the end of an address and indicate which country they come from.* *In this example: Australia, Italy and Germany.*

You will notice that once you have typed in an address, Internet Explorer will remember that you have been there. If you go back to this website again, you will only need to type in the first few letters into the address bar and it will list the addresses with these letters in. You can then select it from the list displayed.

9.4 Finding information using a search engine

If you do NOT know the web address, you will need to search the Internet to find the information you need. To do this, you need a **search engine**.

Search engines are free and you can access them using the Internet. There are lots to choose from but the most common ones are Google, Yahoo and Ask. They all do the same thing and it is up to you which one you use. The most popular one at the moment is Google.

A search engine allows you to type in key words that describe what you are looking for. For example, let's say we want to make a donation to the British Red Cross and we need to find the website. You might start by searching for: Charities. It will then search through the Web to find web pages that contain information based on the key words you typed in. When it has found all the sites, it will display them all in a list. The list may take up hundreds of pages.

Tips and hints

Even the best search engine doesn't search every single page on the Web. You might want to experiment with a couple of different search engines to find the one you like the best. The organizations that provide these search engines are commercial businesses so they will all tell you that theirs is the best.

1 *Open Internet Explorer, if it is not open already.*

2 *Type www.google.co.uk into the address bar. The Google home page will now load.*

3 *Type the word: 'Charity' into the box as shown. Notice that as you start to type the word, Google will predict what it is you are searching for and will show you a list of options. If you see what you want in this list you can click on it. Alternatively, just carry on typing your search words.*

4 *Click on the button for 'Pages from the UK'. This should mean that you only get websites based in the UK, although others do get through sometimes.*

5 *Click on the 'Google Search' button. After a few seconds it will show the results pages listing all of the websites that contain information about charities.*

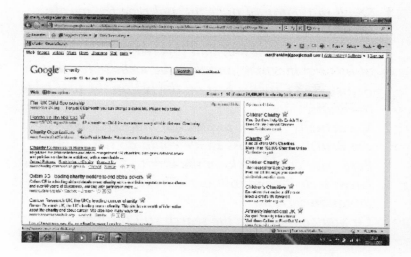

This page shows the first 10 websites that contain information that meet your key words. It also has some sponsored links, to businesses that have paid Google so that their websites will appear on this page. These are the ones in pink at the top and down the right-hand side of the screen.

Each website shown on the results page can be opened by clicking on it. You can read what it says about the website and use this to decide whether it is worth clicking on or not.

In the top right-hand corner you will see how many pages it has found. In this case it has found 24,000,000 pages. This is sometimes called the number of **hits**. It would take years to search through all of these, so we need to narrow down the search.

1 *Scroll to the top of the page and type the words: 'British Red Cross' into the box and click on 'Search'. You will find that this reduces the number of hits significantly, and that the website for the British Red Cross is first on the list on the first page of results.*

2 *We actually wanted to find out how to donate to the British Red Cross so we could do two things here. You could click on the link to the British Red Cross website and follow the hyperlinks to the donation section.*

Or you could refine the search still further:

3 *Type the words: '"British Red Cross" + donation' exactly as shown.*

4 *Press ENTER. The results page will now show a direct link to the donations web page of the British Red Cross website.*

Hints and tips

Putting words inside speech marks means that it will only show websites that contain those words in that sequence. Using the + sign means that it will only include sites that also contain the word 'donation'.

9.5 How to tell if a website is trustworthy

Just because a website is listed by a search engine, does not mean that it contains the information you need, or that the information is correct. Anyone can put information onto a website and there are plenty of strange people out there!

It is not always easy to tell how reliable a website is, but there are some general guidelines you can use:

- *Only rely on websites if they are from organizations or businesses that you already know and trust.*
- *Check for an 'About Us' link to see if you can find out who is responsible for the site.*
- *Check the name of the site. If it is a .gov site for example, you know that it has come from the government (whether you trust it or not is up to you!). If it is .co.uk it could be from anyone.*
- *Most sites are trying to sell you something, so you need to be as cynical as you would be if confronted with a pushy salesman in a shop!*
- *Some websites are what is known as secure sites. There is more information on this in Chapter 15.*

9.6 Dead links and redirection

It is quite common to click on a hyperlink and not to get the page you want. This might be for a number of reasons. The web page might no longer exist, or the link might have been set up incorrectly. These are sometimes called **dead links** as they don't take you anywhere. You will most likely get a message on the screen saying that the web page has not been found.

- *If this happens, click on 'Back'.*

This will take you back to the page that you linked from. It is worth trying again, as sometime you just get a bad connection. If you try again and you get the same message, then the link is probably dead and there is nothing you can do about it.

Sometimes you will be redirected to another website. Sometimes this is for genuine reasons, as the website may have been moved to a different address. Sometimes, it is an advertising ploy to take you to a site that then tries to sell you something. A bit like dead links, all you can do is:

▶ *Click on 'Back' or click on the cross to close the window.*

9.7 Common features of websites

As you will soon discover, every website you visit looks different. At first it can be difficult to find your way around some websites. However, many websites have similar features that you should look out for. For example, on many websites:

▶ *The links to other pages are either across the top of the page or down the left or right-hand side.*
▶ *A registration process is required, usually requiring your email address and a password.*
▶ *You may have to fill in a form to register with the website.*

- *Where the website has masses of information there will be a **browse** or **search** facility to help you find what you are looking for.*
- *There may be the opportunity to **download** things, which means that you can take things like music or software from their sites and put them onto your computer.*

Throughout the rest of this book you will need to use the skills learnt in this chapter. We do use some websites as examples, although we should point out that we are not endorsing these sites and there will always be plenty of others to choose from. We would encourage you to find your own websites either on recommendation from others, or perhaps ones you have seen advertised. Alternatively, you can find suitable sites by typing appropriate search words into a search engine such as Google.

IMPORTANT THINGS TO REMEMBER FROM THIS CHAPTER

1 *The World Wide Web is made up of billions of pages of information grouped into websites.*

2 *You access the Web using a web browser. One common browser is Internet Explorer.*

3 *If you know the web address of the website you are looking for you can type this straight into the address bar in Internet Explorer.*

4 *Websites are made up of many web pages. The first page you look at is usually called the home page.*

5 *Web pages are linked together using hyperlinks. By clicking on a hyperlink you will move between pages. Hyperlinks can be attached to anything, e.g. text or pictures.*

6 *You can spot the hyperlinks because the pointer will change to a hand when you hold the mouse over it.*

7 *Web addresses use some common endings, e.g. .com, .co.uk, .gov. These indicate what type of website it is, e.g. a business or government site.*

8 *You can use a search engine such as Google to search the Web. It will list all the web pages that contain references to the words that you choose to search on.*

9 *You can be more precise with your search words, e.g. by using speech marks and the + sign, to reduce the list of websites that Google finds for you.*

10 *Sometimes websites do not work either because they have moved or because the address is wrong. Sometime you get redirected to a different site to the one you wanted.*

10

....

Keeping organized when using the Web

In this chapter you will learn
- *how to revisit websites you have been to before*
- *how to save websites in a 'favourites' list*
- *how to change your 'home page'*
- *how to have several web pages open at the same time*
- *how to view your history file*
- *how to delete your history file*

10.1 Introduction

In Chapter 9 we looked at how you could find websites either by typing in the web address, or by using a search engine. What you will probably find is that there are some websites that you want to use over and over again. If this is the case, you want to be able to get back to them quickly. Internet Explorer keeps a record of the web pages that you visit. This is called your **history file**. This chapter will look at how you can use the history file to revisit websites. It will also show you how you can create a list of favourite websites – the ones that you will visit the most often.

10.2 Revisiting websites using the address bar

This history file stores the address that you type into the **address bar**. This can be very useful if you want to revisit a website as it saves you having to remember the address. After a while the list can get quite long.

To see how it works:

1 *Open Internet Explorer, if it is not open already.*
2 *Type an address into the address bar, e.g. www.bbc.co.uk.*
3 *After a few seconds, the BBC home page will open.*

So far in this book, we have been to the Oxfam website and to the Google website. You might have been to a few other websites too while you have been experimenting. All these websites will be saved in your history file.

4 *Click on the small arrow at the far right-hand side of the address bar as shown. A list will appear, showing the website addresses that you have typed in.*

5 *To go back to any of these sites, all you have to do is move the mouse over it so that it is highlighted, and then click on it.*

Hints and tips

If something is highlighted it means it has been selected. If you move the mouse up and down on this list you can see how the website that is highlighted changes as you move the mouse.

10.3 Saving websites into a favourites list

The problem with using the address bar to get back to websites you have been to before is that you still have to find the one you want in amongst what could be a long list of sites. If you find a website that you know that you will want to use again, you can save it into a special list, called your **favorites**. (Notice the American spelling.) The idea is that you should only put a small(ish) number of websites into your favourites list. These would be the ones that you visit most often.

Hints and tips

The idea of the favourites is to make it quicker and easier go to a website that you are going to use regularly. If you put too many websites in your favourites list, it defeats the object because the list gets too long.

In this example, we will put the BBC website into the favourites list.

1 *Open the BBC website, either by typing www.bbc.co.uk or by clicking on the little arrow and finding it in the list.*
2 *Click on the icon that contains a small gold star with a green cross on it. This is called 'Add to favorites'.*
3 *Click on 'Add to favorites'. A new window will now open in the middle of the screen:*

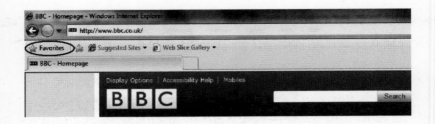

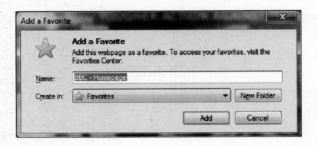

4 *Notice that the Name has been put in automatically – you can type over this with a new name if you like.*

5 *Click on the 'Add' button. The BBC website is now saved in your favourites.*

6 *You can now go to this website at any time by clicking on 'Favorites'. This screen will now be displayed:*

7 *Click on 'Favorites'. A list of every website that you have saved as a favourite is now displayed. In this example there are a few listed, and you can see the BBC website at the bottom of this list. On your computer, you might only have the BBC website in the list.*

8 *To go back to the BBC website, highlight it in the list and click on it. You might want to test this out by changing to another website, and then following these steps to get back to the BBC website.*

10.4 Changing your home page

As you have seen, when you first click on Internet
Explorer, a web page opens up. This is called your
home page. The page it opens will depend on how
you (or the shop) set the computer up in the first place.
You might want to change this to something else.

You usually set your home page to the website that you
use most often, like your email website, or perhaps the
search engine you use most often.

1 *Go to the website that you would like to set as your home page.*
2 *Click on the little arrow next to the icon of the little house as shown:*

3 *Select 'Add or Change Home page'.*
4 *Click on 'Use this page as your only home page'.*
5 *Click on the 'Yes' button. The next time you open Internet Explorer, it will now open this page automatically.*

10.5 Opening several web pages at the same time

Internet Explorer 8 has **tabs** that let you have more than one page open at the same time. This can be quite useful if you want to keep a page open and then go off and view a different page. You can actually have quite a few pages open at the same time if you want to.

To open a new tab:

1 *Click on the new tab icon as shown or you can press CTRL + T.*

2 *A new page will now open that will look like this:*

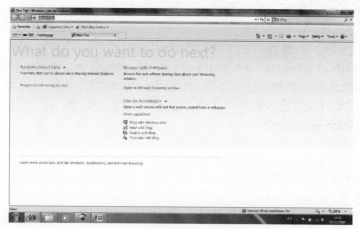

3 *Type the web address of the page that you want to view into the address bar. For example, to open the Oxfam website: type www.oxfam.co.uk. You have now got two pages open: the BBC and Oxfam. You can flick between the two by clicking on the appropriate tab.*

You can close an individual page by clicking on the cross in the tab.

If you close Internet Explorer using the cross in the top right-hand corner, it will close all of your tabs.

Hints and tips

Having too may tabs open can get confusing. Note that the address that is displayed in the address bar relates to whatever tab is currently selected.

10.6 Viewing and deleting websites in your history file

Every website that you visit is automatically saved in a list called your history file. As we have seen, this can be quite useful as you can revisit websites without having to remember the address. However, the history file can get very big. The disadvantage of this is that when you click on the little arrow in the address bar to view the list, it is very long and you can't find what you are looking for.

Another problem is that sometimes you end up on a website that you did not mean to visit, and you might want to delete it from your history file. For example, there are some risks involved with using the Internet, like viruses that can cause problems on your computer, or **spyware** that records what you are doing. Sometimes you get linked to pornographic sites. If you end up on any of these websites, you might want to delete them from the history file.

To view your history file:

1 *Click on 'Favorites'*
2 *Click on 'History'.*
3 *The history file is organized into days and weeks. In this example, you can see where it says 'Today'. This lists all the sites visited on this computer today.*
4 *To view it, click on 'Today'. The sites are now listed.*
5 *To go back to any of these sites, highlight the website and click on it in the list.*
6 *To delete any of these sites from the history file, highlight the website you want to delete and right click on it to open its shortcut menu. In this case, a menu will appear with the options to 'Expand' or 'Delete'.*
7 *Click on 'Delete'. This now removes that website from your history file, and it will not appear in the address bar when you click on the little arrow.*

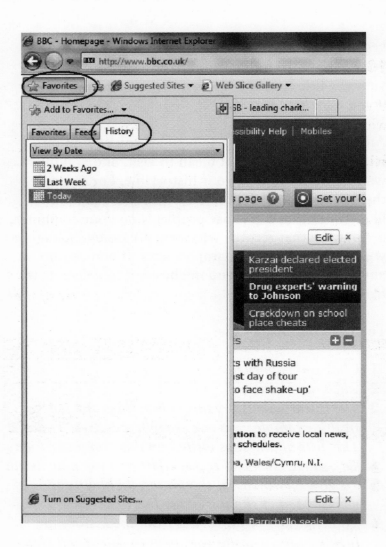

10.7 Deleting your entire history file

If you want find that your address bar has got too full
with old addresses, you can clear the list and start again.

Hints and tips

> You should use your 'Favorites' to save websites
> that you definitely want to go back to again. This
> means that you can safely delete your history file
> from time to time without losing the addresses of
> your favourite websites.

1 *Select 'Tools' near the top right-hand corner of the
   screen as shown.*

2 *Select Options from the menu.*
3 *On the 'General' tab, which should be open, click
   on the 'Delete' button as shown.*
4 *Click on the 'Delete' button on the next screen.
   It may take a few seconds or even minutes to delete
   the history file. When it has finished, this screen
   will disappear.*
5 *Click on 'OK'.*

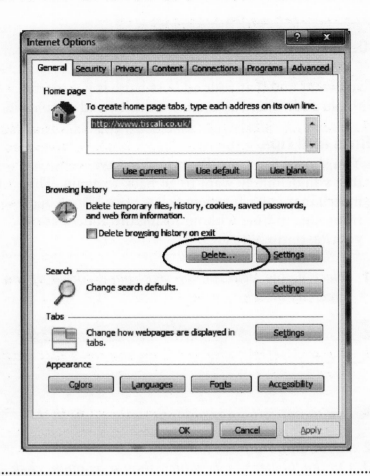

Hints and tips

Notice the 'Settings' button next to 'Delete' in the Browsing History area. If you click this it will open a panel where you can set the amount of space to be used for storing History files, and the number of days to keep files in it. Setting these to low values will reduce the quantity of History information.

IMPORTANT THINGS TO REMEMBER FROM THIS CHAPTER

1 *Internet Explorer remembers the web addresses that you have typed and stores them in the address bar. This is useful if you want to revisit them.*

2 *If you type the first few letters of a web address that you have visited before, it will be shown in a list and you can click on it there.*

3 *The list of visited websites can get very long, if you have high history settings.*

4 *You can put websites into your 'favorites' list. When you want to revisit them you can select them from the favorites list.*

5 *Keep your favorites list well organized so that it is easy to get to the websites that you visit the most often.*

6 *Every time you start your browser, it will load your home page. You can set this to anything you, e.g. your email provider.*

7 *You can open several websites at the same time and flick between them using the 'tabs' across the top of the page.*

8 *Every website that you visit is stored in your history file. You can look at the file to find a web address if you want to revisit it.*

9 *The history file can get very large if you have high settings.*

10 *You can delete individual entries from the history file or delete it all in one go.*

11

Making phone calls over the Internet

In this chapter you will learn
- *how to download Internet phone software*
- *how to make phone calls over the Internet*
- *how to make video calls over the Internet*

11.1 Introduction

When your computer is connected to the Internet, you are part of a massive collection of computers all communicating with each other. It is possible to communicate using text, voice and video with anybody who is connected. Remember that the Internet works on the same basis the telephone system – that is, that information is passed around through wires, cables and satellites.

In the same way that text and images are transferred around the Internet, you can also use it to transmit your voice.

You will need to download some extra software to enable you to do this and, to access most of these efficiently, you will need a broadband connection otherwise it may be too slow.

11.2 What is VOIP?

VOIP stands for Voice Over Internet Protocol, which is computer-speak for the ability to make telephone calls using the Internet. This means that you use your computer like a phone. You talk into your computer at your end and someone else on his or her computer at the other end can hear you and talk to you. If you have a **webcam,** it is also possible to see the person you are talking to and for them to see you. If you are both using the same VOIP website, the phone calls are completely free, even if the person you are talking to is in another country.

For this to work, you do need a broadband Internet connection, a webcam (which will usually have a microphone built in) and some speakers. If you plan to do this a lot, you can also buy an Internet phone, which means that rather than talking into a microphone, you can have a normal hand-held phone. You may prefer a headset which does the same thing but keeps your hands free. You may need to go back to Chapter 2 to find out how to add these to your computer system if you do not have them already.

11.3 Downloading the VOIP software (Skype)

There are different websites that you can get VOIP from. This section will be using a popular one called **Skype**. The first thing you need to do is download the Skype software onto your computer. You will also need to have someone with a computer and a webcam and Skype at the other end so you have got someone to talk to once the download is complete.

This is the first example in this book of having to download software from the Internet. The process of downloading software is normally very simple and pretty much the same for any software. Note that with large programs, downloading can take some minutes, even on a fast broadband connection.

1 *Open Internet Explorer.*

2 *Type www.skype.com into the address bar. The Skype home page will now open.*

3 *Click on the tab for 'download', if you are not on it already, and click 'download now'.*

4 *After you have done this, you will see a screen that looks like this. Click on 'Run'.*

5 *You might get another screen asking if you are sure you want to run it. Click 'Run' again if this happens.*

6 *It may take a few minutes to download the software. You will see a progress bar that shows roughly how long this will take.*

7 *When the download is complete, Click 'Run'.*

8 *Another screen will now be displayed. You will need to click to accept the terms of the licence by ticking the box and then click 'Install'.*

9 *The next screen you see will ask you whether you want to install a Google toolbar. We don't. Clear the tick box and click 'Next'.*

10 *Click on 'Start Skype'. You will now be connected to the Skype website so that you can make phone*

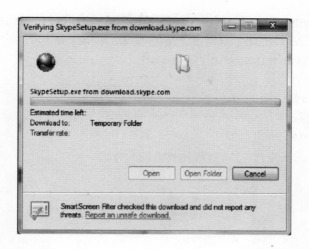

calls. You will not need to go through this process
again as Skype is now installed on your computer.
11 *Close down the Skype website by clicking on the*
cross. We have closed it down, just so we can
see how to open it up again!

11.4 Setting up a Skype user name and password

1 *To open Skype, click on the 'Start' icon.*
2 *Select 'All programs'.*
3 *Find 'Skype' in the list and click on it.*

Hints and tips

When you put new software onto your computer
it usually goes at the end of the list of programs in
the Start menu. It may also have created a shortcut
to it on your desktop.

The main Skype screen will now be displayed. The first thing you need to do is register with Skype and set up your **user name** and **password**.

4 *Click on 'Don't have a Skype name?'*
5 *Complete the form with your details like the example shown and click on 'Next'. Like email, because lots of people use Skype, you might not get the Skype name that you want. If this happens, you will be asked to fill the form in again with another name.*
6 *Make a note of the 'Skype name' that you have chosen.*
7 *There is another form to fill in with your email details. Complete the form as shown and click on 'Sign in'.*

11.5 Making a phone call using Skype

This is the part where you need someone to call and you need to know their Skype address. If you do not know their Skype address you search for it by clicking on 'Search for Skype user'. It is probably easier to phone them up and ask them what it is!

The next time you use Skype it will automatically pick up your settings, although you will have to type in your password. Skype will now take you through a little test routine to check that everything is working. You need to follow the instructions that you are given on the screen.

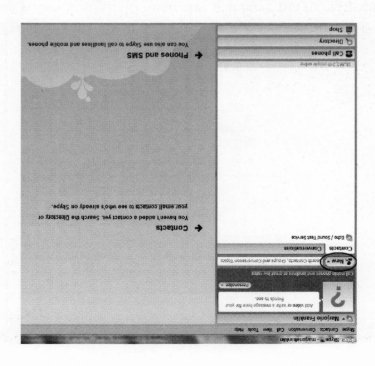

1 Click on the 'New' button in the top left-hand
   corner and select 'New contact'.
2 Type in the Skype name of the person you want to
   contact. Skype will now search its directory to try
   and find the person you are looking for.
3 When you find the right person, click to add them
   to your contacts list. All your Skype contacts will be
   displayed in the main window. In this case there is
   just one contact (the one you have just added):
4 Now click on the 'Contacts' tab and click on this
   person's Skype name.
5 A smaller window will open in the centre of the
   screen. Click on the green phone and it will dial this
   person's number.

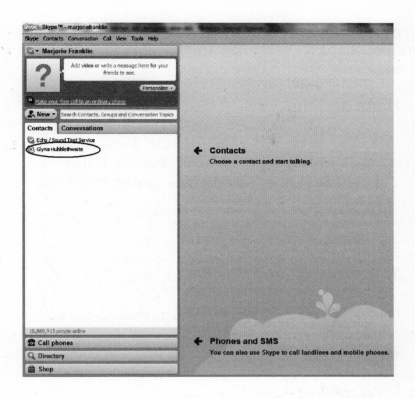

6 *If they are online, they will answer and you will hear their voice coming out of your speakers. You can now talk to them as if it were a normal phone call. If they are not there you will get a message telling you that they have not answered. Note that there is an icon next to each of your contacts indicating their current status, which might be online or offline.*

7 *To end the call, click on the red phone symbol at the bottom.*

If someone calls you using Skype, you will hear your computer ringing and you will need to click on the green phone symbol to accept the call. When you phone from one Skype user to another like this, the calls are free.

Hints and tips

You can also have text messages using Skype by clicking on the 'Conversations' tab. If the person is online you can have a live conversation. If they are not online they will get the messages next time they log on.

11.6 Video calls

Once you have established a voice connection, you will be given the option to video call with that person if you both have webcams set up on your computer.

Hints and tips

Sending and receiving video images and sound requires broadband Internet speeds. Even with broadband, the sound may break up a bit, or the images may be jerky.

If both webcams are working properly, you should automatically be able to see the person you are talking to on the screen. They should be able to see you to. If this does not work automatically:

1 *Select 'Tools' from the menu across the top.*
2 *Select 'Options'.*

3 *Select 'Video' from the list of options on the left-hand side.*

4 *Make sure the 'Enable Skype Video' box is ticked.*

5 *Make sure the 'Start my video automatically' box is ticked.*

6 *Click 'Save'. You should now be able to see the person you are talking to.*

7 *To finish either a voice or video call, you need to click on the red phone icon. This is equivalent of putting the phone down.*

8 *If you have finished with Skype it is best to sign out. Select 'Skype' from the menu at the top left of the screen and click on 'Sign out'.*

You can simply leave yourself signed in if you want to.

IMPORTANT THINGS TO REMEMBER FROM THIS CHAPTER

1 *VOIP stands for Voice Over Internet Protocol and describes the facility to make phone called using the Internet.*

2 *One of the most popular providers of a VOIP service is Skype.*

3 *You can use VOIP to communicate using text, voice and video.*

4 *You need broadband access, special software, and either an Internet phone or a microphone and headset or speakers.*

5 *The first thing you need to do is download and set up the free Skype software.*

6 *You have to set yourself up with a Skype name, which has to be unique.*

7 *Skype has an address book feature called 'Contacts' and a directory where you can search for someone if you don't have their Skype name.*

8 *You can send text messages. The person may respond instantly. If not, the messages are there for them next time they go to their Skype account.*

9 *You can make telephone calls in the same way as a normal call. You can use an Internet phone for these, or a headset.*

10 *You can also have a video call if you have a webcam. You will be able to see and hear the person you are talking to.*

12

Chatting over the Internet

In this chapter you will learn
- *how to download and use 'instant messaging' software*
- *how to chat using text, sound and video*
- *how to find and enter public chat rooms*

12.1 Introduction

Emails are a very popular way of communicating, but one of the problems with email is that it is not instant. You send an email, and then you wait for a reply. That might take a few minutes, hours or days. Sometimes you want to be able to have a live conversation with someone where you get an instant response. There are two main ways of doing this:

> ▶ Use **instant messaging (IM) software.** *This enables you to chat with people who you know – they would need to have the same IM software on their*

computer. You can get access to IM software in a number of ways. It is available within Skype or you can download Messenger, which is a Microsoft product. It is also available on the websites of most of the social networking sites such as FaceBook.

▶ *Use a* **chat room***. Generally speaking you don't need any special software to use a chat room, you just log on to a chat room website and you can join in the live conversations that are taking place.*

12.2 Using Skye for instant messaging

As we have already used Skype it makes sense to use the instant messaging facility as an example here. You may choose to download or use other IM software, all of which works in a very similar way to how it works in Skype.

1 *Open the Skype software. If you do not have this, refer to Chapter 11.*

2 *If you signed out from your previous session you will have to sign back in. The following screen is displayed and you will need to type in your Skype name and password and click on 'Sign in'.*

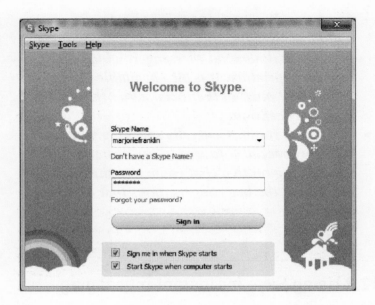

3 *You will now see the main Skye screen that you use to make phone calls.*

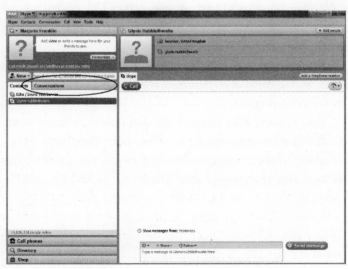

4 *Click on 'Contacts' and select the person you want to chat with. In the example above there is just one person on the list, Glynis Hubblethwaite. Notice that each name has an icon next to it, which indicates the status of the contact. The symbol shown in the example above means that Glynis is not currently logged in. A green tick means that they are on-line now.*

5 *Click on 'Conversations'.*

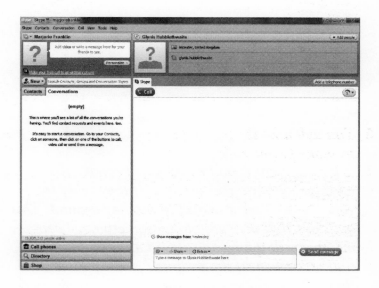

6 *If there has been any previous conversation, you will be able to access them again here. As this is the first time Marjorie has chatted with Glynis using Skype, this shows a message saying it is empty.*

7 *To start chatting, type what you want to say in the box highlighted. You can then either press ENTER or click on the 'Send message' button.*

8 *You will notice that each time you do this, what you have typed is shown in the white space above with the time that you sent the message.*

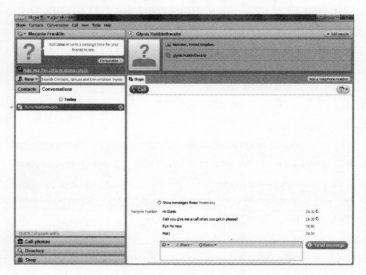

9 *If the recipient is on line they will receive the message within a few seconds. If they reply to you, you will see a small pen moving around. This indicates that they are typing something. Their message will then be displayed after the message that you typed. If the recipient is not on line then they will get the message the next time they open their Skype software on their computer.*

10 *Assuming they are there and that they send you a message, you can then reply to their message and the text conversation or chat goes on in this way.*

11 *If you decide that you would rather talk to them, you can simply click on 'Call' and turn it into a real chat.*

Hints and tips

When text chatting there is sometimes a slight delay between you pressing ENTER and the person at the other end getting the message. It's a bit like a satellite delay when they are doing interviews on the TV!

12.3 Chat rooms

Chat rooms are public websites where you can have **real-time** conversations with people. Some chat rooms are general, where people go in and chat about anything they like. Other chat rooms are themed, which means that the chat is about a specific topic. Some chat rooms are regulated, which means that there is a moderator who keeps an eye on what is being said, in case it gets offensive. Others are not supervised, and anything goes.

There are thousands of chat rooms on the Internet covering every possible theme. You can find a chat room by using a search engine and typing in suitable search words, e.g. 'chat room + gardening'. Also, many well-known websites have a chat room facility, e.g. Google and Yahoo both operate chat rooms on a range of themes. Also, many charities now have chat rooms where you can find people with the same interests and concerns. Many medical and health charities for example, have chat rooms for people affected by illness.

Many chat rooms are of an adult nature although
this is usually made obvious before you enter it.
These tend to be unregulated so if you are easily
offended, steer clear.

This example will use Yahoo chat rooms. For this
to work you need to download Yahoo Messenger
software. This enables you to get onto the Yahoo chat
rooms and can also be used as an alternative to Skype
as a way of sending instant messages to your friends.

1 *Type chat.yahoo.com into
   the address bar of Internet
   Explorer.*

2 *Click on the links to
   'Download' and follow the
   instructions to download
   the software onto your
   computer. This will take a
   few minutes depending on
   the speed of your Internet
   connection.*

3 *When it is complete the
   new software will open
   automatically. It will
   subsequently be available
   either from a shortcut placed
   on the desktop, or from the
   Start, All Programs menu.*

4 *You will have to register
   with Yahoo to get a Yahoo
   ID before you can start*

chatting. Click on 'Get a new Yahoo! ID'. You will be asked to complete an on-line form. This involves the usual information including a name, password and email address. They may also ask for gender and date of birth. You need to fill these in, but you don't have to give the right information!

5 You then go back to the log-on screen to type in the Yahoo ID and password that you have just created. The main screen will look like this. You may want to experiment with some of the options here as they will be quite similar to Skype in terms of adding contacts and sending text messages.

6 To get into a chat room, select 'Messenger' from the menu at the top.

7 *Select Yahoo! Chat and 'Join a room'. A list of rooms will now be displayed:*

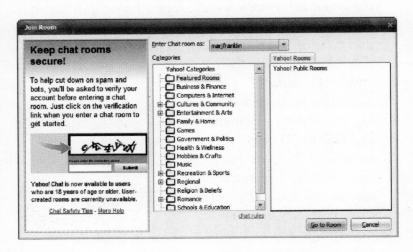

8 *Click on the 'Categories' and it will show you what rooms are available and how many people are in them. The main problem with chat rooms can be finding like-minded people who are online at the same time as you. You may enter a few rooms to find people who you want to chat to. The names of the rooms usually give you an idea as to what the chat is about.*

9 *Double click to enter a room of your choice. You will then see a screen that looks like this. On the right you can see the list of people who are in the room and the conversation thread is shown to the left of this.*

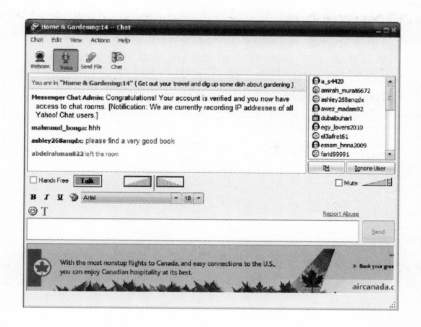

10 *To start chatting, type into the white rectangular box near the bottom of the screen and either press ENTER or click on 'Send'. Your message will appear in the main window. Other people in the room may then reply to it.*

11 *You may receive messages from people asking you if you want a* **personal chat**. *This means that you would enter into a one-to-one chat with that person. You can accept or decline this offer.*

12 *When you have finished chatting, you can click on the cross, or log out and a message is shown on screen to show that you have left the room.*

Hints and tips

Chat rooms are used for quite a lot of flirting so you may get some unwanted (or wanted) attention in chat rooms. There is more on using the Internet for meeting new people in Chapter 25, including advice on keeping safe.

IMPORTANT THINGS TO REMEMBER FROM THIS CHAPTER

1 *Instant messaging is a way of communicating in real time with someone on another computer anywhere in the world. It uses text.*

2 *Chat rooms are websites where you can have text-based conversations with people inside a virtual room.*

3 *There are a number of providers of Instant messaging (IM) services including Skype.*

4 *You type in what you want to say and send the message. The person at the other end responds and a conversation develops.*

5 *Chat rooms allow real-time conversations with a number of people at the same time and work in the same way as IM.*

6 *Chat rooms are available from a number of providers and tend to be based around themes, e.g. for particular hobbies or age groups.*

7 *The idea of chat rooms is that you can meet like-minded people who you might not otherwise get the chance to meet in real life.*

8 *Some chat rooms are 'moderated' by a person who checks that the conversations are appropriate. In other chat rooms, anything goes.*

9 *You can have a 'personal chat' (pc) in a chat room. To do this you can request a pc or you may receive a request to have a pc.*

10 *Chat rooms can get quite lively and many people use them to flirt and meet new people. If in doubt, click on the cross and try another one.*

13

....

Getting involved with online communities

In this chapter you will learn
- *how to take part in ongoing discussions using a 'forum'*
- *how to pursue specialist interests via 'Newsgroups'*
- *how to read and contribute to 'wikis'*
- *how to view 'social networking sites'*

13.1 Introduction

Millions of people now use the Internet on a daily basis. As well as using the Internet to find information, more and more people are now adding their own contributions. For example, as well as using the BBC website to read news articles, people are now encouraged to have their say about news items, to **post** comments and to get into discussions with other visitors to the website. Whole communities have developed on the Internet. For example, if you had a particular interest in gardening, you would be able to find **forums** where gardeners meet online to take part in discussions and share information.

Social networking sites like MySpace, Facebook, Twitter and Bebo have become very popular. This is where people create an online profile of themselves for everyone to view. Finally, there is the phenomenon known as a **wiki**, an example being Wikipedia. This is an encyclopaedia that is written and constantly updated by anyone on the Internet who feels that they know enough to contribute to it.

13.2 Forums

A forum or message board is like an online notice board. Like a real notice board, users can post up messages for other people to read. Other users can then make comments about these messages and a discussion develops. Hundreds of thousands of forums exist on the Internet covering every imaginable topic. Many websites carry forums to let people post messages about the website.

They are a bit like chat rooms, but the difference is that they are not in real-time. That means that you post your message, and then wait a while for responses to come back.

You can find forums by typing suitable search words into a search engine, e.g. 'forum + genealogy'. Alternatively, you will find forums on many of your favourite websites. For example, the BBC has a large number of forums covering all sorts of topics such as the news, gardening, and money matters.

1 Type *www.bbc.co.uk/gardening into the address bar of Internet Explorer.*
2 *To get into the gardening message board, click on 'Message Board'. You may need to scroll down first to find the link.*

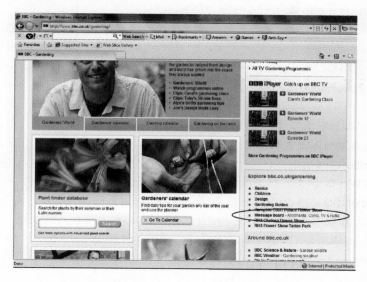

3 *The next page will show you some of the main discussion topics that are ongoing. You can click on any of these to take part. For example, to get involved in the discussion on 'Gardening on TV and radio', click on the link.*

4 *The next screen will show you all of the posts, which are messages that have been left by other people. This site has lots of posts that go over several pages. To read a post, click on it.*

5 *Most forums let you read the messages without having to register, but ask you to register your details if you want to reply or to start new discussions. You need to register with the BBC website if you want to do this. Follow the links to 'Register for membership'. This is a standard form like the other ones you have had to fill in*

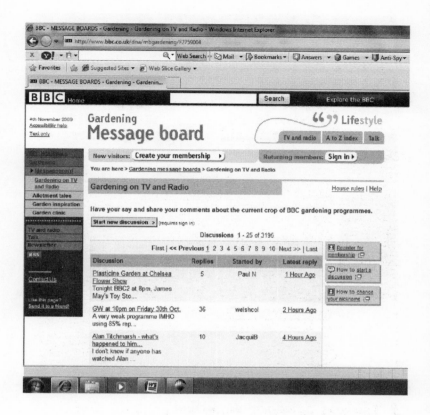

while using the Internet. You will need to put in your email address, as they will send you an email, which you must respond to in order to activate your membership.

6 *Once your membership is activated you can post your own messages by clicking on 'Reply to this message'.*

7 *To start a new discussion topic, click on the general topic, e.g. 'Garden clinic'. To get back to this page, click the 'Back' button in Internet Explorer.*

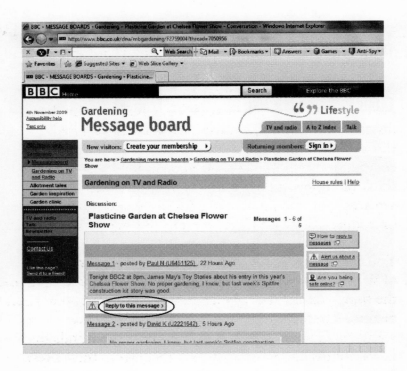

8 *Click on the link to 'Garden clinic'.*
9 *Click on 'Start new discussion'.*
10 *Give your message a catchy title, type the message and click 'Post message'.*
11 *You can follow the replies by clicking on 'My discussions'.*

Hints and tips

There are so many discussions on the go, that you need to give it a meaningful and interesting title to get people to take part in yours.

13.3 Newsgroups

Newsgroups are very similar to forums in that they are electronic message boards. They were originally distributed by email, but can now also be accessed through the Web. There are thousands of newsgroups covering every possible topic and subtopic that you can think of. Some of the topics are very specific, so they are a way of finding people who share your interests, or finding advice on issues even if they are very specific.

You can get access to newsgroups in a number of ways. You can use a search engine and type in the topic you are looking for, e.g. 'newsgroups + health'. Alternatively, the two big search engine websites, Google and Yahoo, both **host** thousands of newsgroups, and you can access them from their sites. To find a Google newsgroup:

1 *Type http://groups.google.com/ into the address bar of Internet Explorer.*
2 *You will be prompted to log in. If you have already signed up for Google services such as Google Mail, you can use the same log on details here. If not, you will have to go register with Google.*

Once you have logged on you will be shown all the categories for the newsgroups. In this example, we will search for a newsgroup that covers the fairly specific topic of pension annuities.

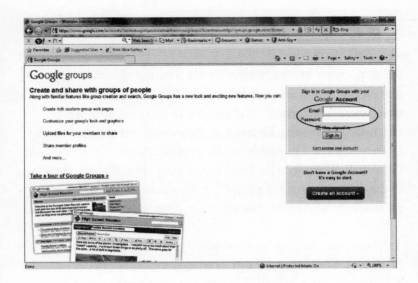

3 *Type annuities into the search box and click on 'Search for a group'.*

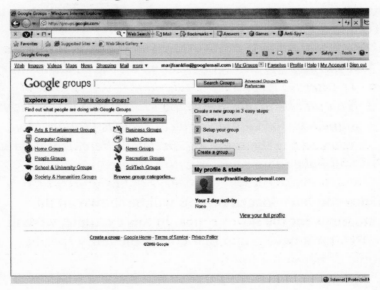

4 *The results are listed and you can see all the groups with a brief description as to what is covered. In this case, you can also select by category or look through the listings just as you would with a normal Google search.*

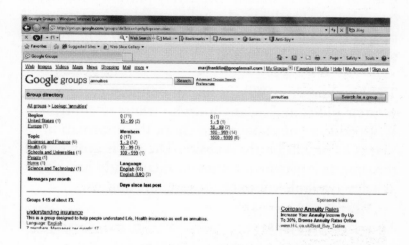

5 *Click on one of the links. The messages will now be shown and can be read.*
6 *To reply to a message, click on the 'Reply' link at the bottom of the message. Type in your comment and click 'Send'.*

Hints and tips

Remember that these are discussion groups, which anyone can contribute to. The opinions expressed in them are those of the person and should not be taken as fact.

13.4 Wikis

A wiki is a website that lets users read, add and edit the content of the website. These are becoming very popular as a way of collaboratively putting information on websites. The logic of a wiki is that with so many people reading and editing the material, it is more likely to be correct and unbiased.

The best known is Wikipedia, an online encyclopaedia, written and edited by anyone who wants to contribute. Wikipedia employs people to check the information that is being put on the website. The site is growing all the time as it gets better known. It currently has 1.7m articles available covering all sorts of subjects.

To view Wikipedia:

1 *Type www.wikipedia.org into the address bar of Internet Explorer.*
2 *Type what it is you want to read or contribute to in the search box. In this example we are looking at 'Inheritance tax'. The article on this subject is then displayed.*
3 *You can simply read this article, or because it is a wiki, you can edit it. To do this, click on the link to 'edit this page' on the section that you want to make changes to.*
4 *On this page, you can edit the text content on the article. When you have finished, click on 'Save page'. The changes you have made will be shown instantly.*

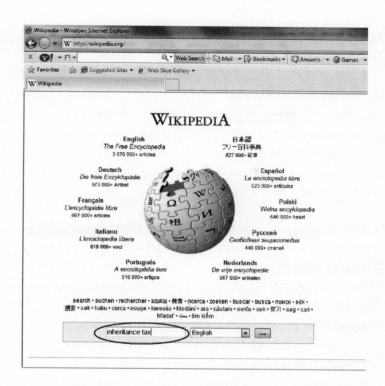

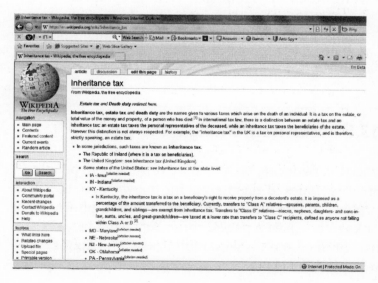

You must first register as a contributor before you can add or edit the articles at Wikipedia. Your should be careful not to break copyright rules or write anything libellous. You will be held reponsible for what you write as your IP address is recorded by Wikipedia. That all sounds a bit serious, but it's to stop people making silly changes – after all, millions of pople might now read the changes you have just made!

13.5 Social networking websites

Social networking websites are those where people create profiles of themselves for the world to see. The profile can include personal information, photographs, links to other web pages, comments from viewers, lists of likes and dislikes and information about relationships. As well as viewing other people's profiles, you can also create your own. These sites are very popular among young people, but older people are also getting involved. Two of the best known sites are MySpace and Facebook. Twitter, which is very popular at the moment, is a cross between a social networking site and a blog, where people write brief messages about what they are doing right now.

Many people use social networking sites as a way of making contact with new people with a view to meeting up in the 'real world' as well as the 'virtual world'.

1 *To view profiles of people of a similar age, type www.myspace.com into the address bar of Internet Explorer.*
2 *Click on 'Browse'. This takes you to the area for meeting people.*

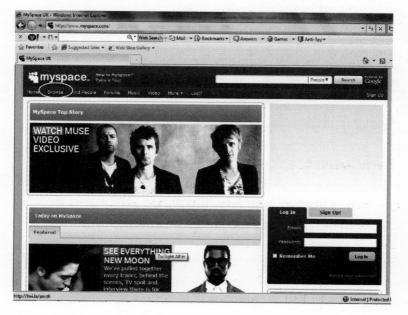

3 *Set the gender, age and location criteria to filter out the thousands of profiles, so that you will only be shown those that you may be interested in.*

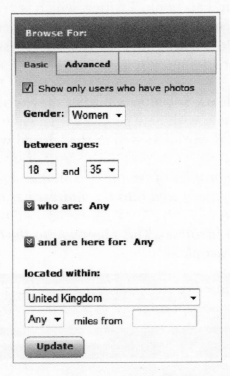

4 *Make your selections and click 'Update'. You will now be shown a list of profiles that meet your criteria.*

5 *Click on any of the pictures to link to their profile. Once in their profile you can add comments or send messages to the person.*

IMPORTANT THINGS TO REMEMBER FROM THIS CHAPTER

1 *There are many different ways in which you can interact with people over the Internet. In online communities you can communicate with people who you will never meet in the real world.*

2 *A 'forum' is like an online notice board where you can post messages and reply to other people's messages.*

3 *Forums tend to be set up for specific topics, often linked to hobbies and pastimes, e.g. on gardening or motoring.*

4 *When you leave a message this is called a 'post'. People will respond to your post and a 'thread' will develop.*

5 *Newsgroups are similar to forums and usually cover very specific topic areas. Some have a person who acts as moderator.*

6 *A wiki is a collaborative website where as well as reading information, you can add your own and edit what other people have written.*

7 *The best known wiki is Wikipedia, which is an online encyclopaedia.*

8 *Facebook and MySpace are social networking websites where you can create a profile of yourself and communicate with other people.*

9 *You can use social networking sites to send messages, display information about yourself and share contact details between friends.*

10 *Social networking sites are popular as they are a way of making links between mutual friends and expanding your circle of contacts.*

14

Reading and writing blogs

In this chapter you will learn
- *what a blog is*
- *how to find blogs that you might want to read*
- *how to read and comment on blogs*
- *how to set up a blogging site of your own*
- *how to write a blog*

14.1 Introduction

A **blog** (short for web log) is a web page written by an individual or group of people, usually in the style of a journal that contains regular entries (like a diary). Each entry is called a **post**. Posts are dated and shown in reverse chronological order. The information in a blog could be anything from the day-to-day life of the **blogger**, through to information on particular topics and themes. Many blogs are text only, though they can contain images, movies and sounds. A blog usually reflects the personality of the blogger and may contain links to other websites that the blogger is interested in.

Some blogs have become extremely popular with millions of people reading them on a regular basis. Some people have become famous from writing blogs, and some famous people now have blogs. Twitter is worth a special mention at this stage as it is so popular. The idea of this is that you write short messages telling people what you are doing and thinking right now. It is sometimes called **micro-blogging** as you are not supposed to write much.

14.2 Finding blogs to read

In common with anything else on the Internet, your start point could be to use a search engine to find blogs on themes that you are interested in. For example, typing 'blog + classical music' into a search engine will give you thousands of potential blogs to read. Many of your favourite websites may also carry blogs. For example, many leading newspapers and TV stations have blogs. This blog is from political journalist Nick Robinson:

This is a fairly typical blog. It has the latest entry at the top and links down the sides to other blog entries, to topics being discusses, and to other websites that the blogger thinks you might be interested in.

Another way of finding a blog is to use a specialist bloggers site. One of the most popular is Blogger, which is part of Google's network of websites.

1 *Type www.blogsearch.google.com into the address bar of Internet Explorer.*
2 *You use this like you would for a normal Google search although you will see that it is set up to look for blogging websites only.*
3 *There is a search box into which you type your key words. Type in the subject that you are interested in, e.g. travel, and click on 'Search Blogs'. As with any search, you should try and be as specific as possible with the search words to reduce the number of hits. In this example the search words were 'Travel + Europe' and it produced thousands of potential blogs to read.*

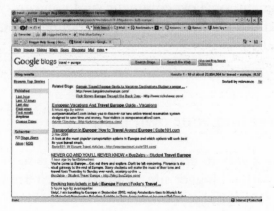

4 *The search results give you a brief description of the contents of the blog. You can scroll through them, and move between the pages until you find one you want to read. Then click on it and the blogger's webpage will open.*

Hints and tips

Many businesses now use blogs to link you to their websites so that they can try and sell you something. Look at the address of the blog before you click on it to decide whether this is the case, and whether you want to go to their site.

Depending on who has created the blog, the web page may either look very professional with lots of **multimedia** content, or it might be very text-heavy. Remember that blogs often reflect the personality of the blogger and some will be better than others. Once you are in the blogger's website, it is just like being in any other website. You can read the text, look at photographs, play videos, etc. Bloggers also invite you to comment on their blogs. There will usually be a link to 'Comment' or 'Post comment' and you can type in what you think about the blog, or comments on the contents.

14.3 Creating your own blog

The easiest way to create your own blog is to register with a blogger site, many of which are free.

The advantage of using a site like Blogger is that you can create a professional looking web page without having to learn how to use any specialist software. We will be using www.blogger.com.

1 Type www.blogger.com into the address bar of Internet Explorer.
2 You will need to sign in using your Google Mail address or if you have not got one, you will need to register now.
3 Click on 'Create a blog'.

4 *Choose a title that will be shown on your blog.*

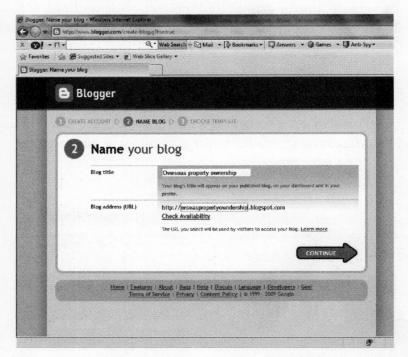

5 *You now need to set up a **URL**, which is the web address that will be allocated to your blog. Then click 'Continue'. In this example the blog is going to be about owning overseas property and the URL will be http://overseaspropertyownershop.blogspot.com.*

6 *You will now be shown a number of templates for the web page that will hold your blog. Take a look through the list and choose the one you like.*

7 *You are now ready to write your blog so click on 'Start blogging'.*

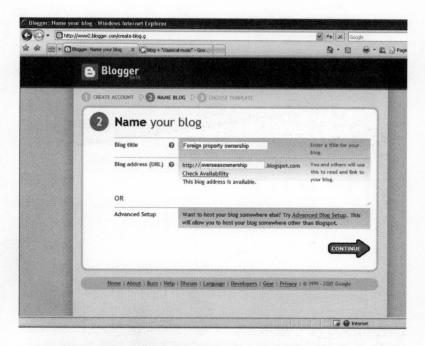

8 *Type in the title for this entry into your blog and type what you want to say into the large box on the screen as shown.*

9 *When you have finished typing, click on 'Publish Post'.*

10 *Click on 'View blog'. Your blog is published for the whole world to read. It should look something like the one at the bottom of the next page.*

Hints and tips

Once your blog is set up you can give your friends this web address and they can type it into Internet Explorer and read your blog.

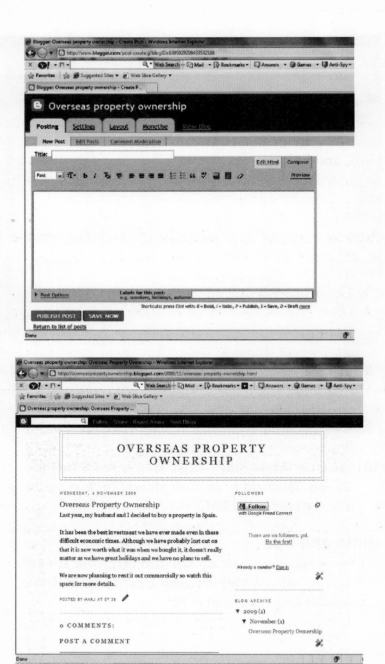

14.4 Developing your blog

At the moment, we have created a fairly basic blog, which contains some text. You may want to develop your blog to include photographs, audio and video clips, and links to other websites. You might also want to put on more personal information about yourself to share with the world.

A useful start point for this is to edit your User Profile to let people know more about you.

1 *Click on 'Customize'.*
2 *Click on 'Dashboard'. From here you can manage your blog including your user profile and all the entries you have written.*
3 *Click on 'Edit profile'.*

In here you can do things like add photographs of yourself, or video clips. You can also tell people more about yourself, your hobbies and interests. Remember that blogging is all about sharing your thought and ideas with the world, and being part of an **online community**.

4 *When, complete, click on 'Save profile'.*
5 *Back on the 'Dashboard', you can also view posts, add new posts, create new blogs, and get access to your user profile. You can also access the 'Help' screens from here to help you with other aspects of blogging.*
6 *When you have finished, make sure that you click on 'Log out' before clicking on the cross to close the website.*
7 *When you want to get back to your blog, type www.blogger.com into the address bar (or you save it into your favourites), and then type in your user name and password.*

Hints and tips

Remember that your blog can be seen by anyone, and be careful about the personal information that you publish on it. Safety on-line is the topic for the next two chapters.

IMPORTANT THINGS TO REMEMBER FROM THIS CHAPTER

1 *Blogs (or web logs) are online diary entries that you make available to everyone via a website.*

2 *You can read other people's blogs or you can write your own. Blogs can be about anything. Some people just record their day-to-day lives while some blogs are on specific topics.*

3 *Blogs can contain words, pictures and videos.*

4 *You can find blogs that you might like to read by doing a search of the Internet. You need to type in the specific details of the type of blogs you are looking for.*

5 *Most blogs invite comments from readers so you can have your own say about something you have read.*

6 *You can create your own blogs. The easiest way to do this is to use one of the blogging websites. You will have to register with the site although most of them are free.*

7 *Blogging websites make it easy for you to set up your blog by offering you predefined layouts for the page.*

8 *Your blogs can consist only of text or as you get more confident, you can start adding other features to your websites such as photographs and video.*

9 *Blogs allow you to set up your personal profile. This can be shared with your readers so that they can get to know more about you.*

10 *Blogs can be used as a way of making new friends and finding like-minded people.*

15

Keeping your personal information safe online

In this chapter you will learn
- *about the risks involved when using the Internet*
- *how you can protect yourself against these risks*
- *advice on buying online*
- *advice on passwords*

15.1 Introduction

The Internet is a global connection of computers with the connections being made by telephone cables and satellites. It all works like the telephone system and logging on to the Internet is a bit like making a telephone call. In fact, your computer has its own number (called an **IP address**), which is transmitted whenever you are online. In the same way that a telephone call can be intercepted, so can any of the information that is transmitted when you are in the Internet.

The Internet is very largely unregulated, and pretty much anyone can get access to it. Unfortunately this means that it is open to abuse. This chapter lists the threats that exist and in each case, explains what you can do about them.

15.2 Phishing and identity theft

Identify theft occurs when someone obtains personal information about you which means that they can pretend to be you, usually for fraudulent reasons. They could buy things from the Internet in your name, or perhaps borrow money or even clear out your bank account.

One of the ways that they can obtain the information is by **phishing** – sending an email claiming to be from your bank. They will ask for personal information including your bank account details, or direct you to a fake website that asks you for this information. These emails can look very convincing.

What to do about it:

▶ *Banks will never email you to ask you for personal information such as PIN codes and passwords. If you are asked for it, don't give it.*
▶ *Make sure that when you are doing any banking over the Internet that the site is secure.* **Secure sites** *have https in the address, display a small padlock*

just to the right-hand side of the address bar and will turn the address bar green:.

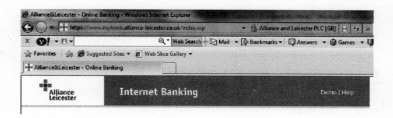

This is the log-on page for the Alliance and Leicester. Notice how the address has the https at the beginning and there is a padlock icon. Do not disclose any personal information unless the site has both of these showing.

15.3 Hacking

Hacking is when someone gains unauthorized access to your computer. They can do this any time you are connected to the Internet. You will not even know that it is happening. Hackers do it for various reasons. Often it is just bored teenagers, but some hackers do it with the intention of getting your personal information.

What to do about it:

▶ *Install a* **firewall.** *This is software and hardware that examines information that is being passed*

*to your computer while you are online. If it finds
something it doesn't like, it will block it. If you are
using Windows you will already have a firewall.
There are lots of different makes of firewall
software available to buy. You can find these
by searching for them on the Internet.*

▶ *Disconnect from the Internet. Only stay online if
you need to be. At other times, log yourself off.
To do this:*

1 *Click on the 'Network and Sharing centre' icon on
the right-hand side of the Taskbar.*

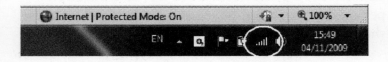

2 *This window will show you all your connections
including any local area networks that you may
have set up. If you are connected using a local area
network then you can disconnect by clicking on it
here and selecting 'Disconnect'.*

3 *If it shows that you are connected directly to the
Internet, you can click on it and then 'Disconnect'.*

4 *To log back on, you click on the same icon in the
toolbar and 'Connect'.*

15.4 Undesirable material

The unregulated nature of the Internet means that you can get access to plenty of undesirable material. Often you will click on a site that you think is perfectly innocent only to find that it contains undesirable content. This may be of particular concern if children have access to your computer.

What to do about it:

▸ *Use your common sense. If you don't like what you see, click on the cross immediately to close the website.*
▸ *Install* **filtering and blocking software.** *This special software allows you to block access to sites that contain undesirable content.*
▸ *Set the 'Content Advisor rating' in Windows 7. This is like the filtering/blocking software mentioned before but is already built into Windows.*

1 *To set the content advisor rating, with Internet Explorer open click on 'Tools' near the top right-hand side of the screen.*
2 *Select 'Internet Options'.*
3 *Click on the 'Content' tab as shown.*
4 *Click on 'Enable'. The following screen is displayed:*

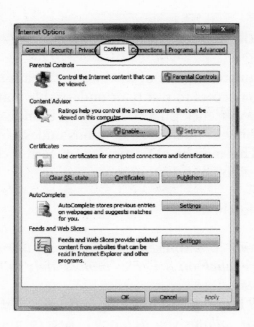

5 *You can now select a rating for each category by moving the slider. In most cases, you will want the slider as far over to the left as you can get it.*

Hints and tips

As there is so much undesirable content on the Internet, these filters are not 100 per cent effective. It is recommended that you buy specialist filtering/ blocking software if you are particularly concerned about it.

There is more information on some of the other security features of Internet Explorer in the next chapter.

15.5 Premium diallers

A **premium dialler** is a piece of software that installs itself onto your computer without you realizing it. The next time you log on to the Internet it will not use your normal number to connect, but will dial a premium rate service charging up to £1.50 a minute. This is legal as the software does not install itself without you knowing it – you will see a message that asks you if you want to install it. However, the message is not clearly worded so you may click 'Yes' not really understanding what you are signing up to.

This is a tricky scam as you often see messages popping up when you are on the Internet, and most of them are fairly benign. You are most likely to encounter a premium dialler scam on download sites. These are sites where you can get free software.

What to do about it:

▸ *Read all messages carefully before clicking 'Yes' whenever you are on the Internet.*
▸ *Phone your telephone company (e.g. BT) and ask them to block all outgoing calls to premium rate numbers.*
▸ *Only use reputable sites.*

15.6 Unreliable sites

Many of the problems described in this chapter come from unreliable sites. But how do you spot a dodgy site? It is not always easy as even bad websites can be made to look good.

What to do about it:

▸ *Don't click on a link to a website that comes from an unsolicited email.*
▸ *Look for a 'real world' presence, preferably an address.*
▸ *Only use sites of well-known businesses or sites that are recommended.*

▶ *Avoid sites that offer free downloads, free movies, free music, free games or* **file-sharing**.

15.7 Buying online

When you buy anything online there is always a danger that the goods will not be delivered, or what is delivered, is not what you ordered.

What to do about it:

▶ *Only buy from trusted websites. This could be the websites of large companies or those that have been recommended by a friend.*

▶ *Keep copies of all receipts. All decent online stores will provide a screen where you can print a copy of your order. Most will also send an email to confirm the order.*

▶ *Check for a real address so that you can contact them if something goes wrong. It is preferable if they are located in the same country as you!*

▶ *Use your common sense. If a deal looks too good to be true – it probably isn't true.*

▶ *Ensure the payment area of the site is secure – look for the https and the padlock symbol.*

▶ *Have a separate credit/debit card that you use for online transactions and only have a small credit limit on it.*

▶ *Use secure payment services such as* **PayPal**. *These provide insurance against non-delivery.*

15.8 Passwords

Passwords usually in combination with a user name are required all over the place. Your computer itself will probably require a user name and password. Email sites, online auctions, chat rooms, etc. all require you to register with a user name and password.

Passwords are very important. There are some rules that you should follow:

▶ *Never give your password to anyone else, ever.*
▶ *Change your password regularly and don't use the same password twice. (This one is tricky as it is difficult to remember them all.)*
▶ *Don't choose something obvious like names, dates of birth, etc. Use combinations of letters and numbers, as they are harder to guess.*
▶ *Don't write passwords down anywhere.*

Don't have nightmares...

Internet crime is increasing and you are never immune to threats even if you take all of the precautions listed in this chapter. However, if you take precautions, the chances of becoming a victim are very small. Remember that millions of people now use the Internet regularly with no problems.

IMPORTANT THINGS TO REMEMBER FROM THIS CHAPTER

1 *Whenever you are connected to the Internet there is a risk that someone could obtain your personal information.*

2 *The level of risk is relatively low and can be minimized by taking a few basic precautions mainly to protect your personal details.*

3 *Identity theft is where a criminal uses personal details about you to their own benefit. This is usually some form of fraud.*

4 *Phishing for bank details is a common way of getting people to disclose their personal details. NEVER give out your bank details in an email.*

5 *Hacking is where someone accesses your computer remotely, that is, via your Internet connection. You can prevent this with a firewall.*

6 *There is a lot of undesirable material on the Internet due to the fact that it is largely unregulated. There are also some scamsters operating online.*

7 *If something appears to be too good to be true then it probably isn't true. You should exercise the same care that you would in the real world.*

8 *You can set up filters and parental controls to prevent most undesirable material being available. If you stumble upon it by accident and don't like what you see, click on the cross and get rid of it.*

9 *Premium diallers are scam websites that redirect your telephone connection to the Internet onto an expensive phone line.*

10 *You should use passwords wherever needed. You should change the password regularly and never disclose it to anyone.*

16

···

Keeping your computer safe from online threats

In this chapter you will learn
- *about the risks to your computer and the information stored on it*
- *how you can protect yourself against these risks*
- *what problems are caused by junk email (spam)*
- *how to create a back-up of important information in case of loss*

16.1 Introduction

Your computer is at risk every time you are on the Internet. It is virtually impossible to avoid picking up a few problems whenever you use the Internet. At one end of the scale, you might find that you get a lot of junk email (**spam**) or **pop-ups**, which are annoying, and clog up your computer, but do not actually damage it. At the other end of the scale, you could pick up a computer virus, which could destroy information and programs stored on your computer. Let's look at the annoying ones first.

16.2 Junk email

Junk email, also known as **spam,** is almost impossible to avoid. Junk emails appear in the inbox of your email software. You didn't ask for it and you don't know the person or organization that sent it. Most of the time, they are just advertising things, particularly Viagra, distinctly dodgy investments and pornographic material.

What do to about it:

- ▶ *Most email software will filter out spam emails for you and put them into a special folder called Spam. However, some will still get through.*
- ▶ *It is possible to minimize the amount of junk mail you get by blocking or reporting it to your service provider. This means that you should not receive any more spam from these organizations again. For example, in Gmail you can click on the 'Report spam' button when you get it:*
- ▶ *If you do not know whom an email is from, delete it without opening it.*
- ▶ *Don't reply to email from spammers.*

The real danger of spam is that email is a very common way to pick up a computer virus, and these can be quite serious, as we will see later on.

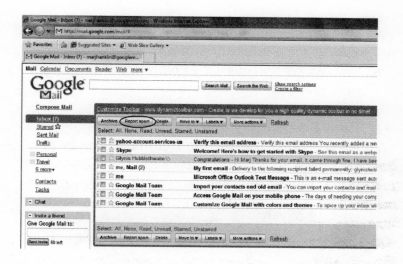

16.3 Pop-ups

Pop-ups are windows that just pop up (appear) when you are using the Internet. Like spam, they are not something that you asked for – they just appear. Most of these pop-ups are just advertising something. Some of them look quite enticing because they tell you that you have won something. This is usually just a trick to get you to visit their website.

Pop-ups are not necessarily bad, but they can be annoying if you get a lot of them. The simple solution to a pop-up is simply to click on the cross and get rid of it.

What to do about it:

▶ *Read the pop-up, as it might be a genuine offer from a reputable company. If not, click on the cross.*

▶ *You can buy pop-up blocking software, which reduces the amount of pop-ups you will get.*
▶ *You can set up Internet Explorer so that it stops most pop-ups:*

1 *Open Internet Explorer.*
2 *Select 'Tools' near the top right-hand corner of the screen.*
3 *Select 'Pop-up Blocker'.*

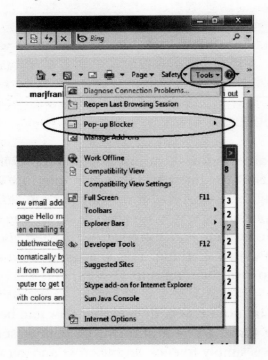

4 *Select 'Turn on Pop-up Blocker'.*
5 *Click on 'OK'. This should now stop most pop-ups from appearing and will warn you when it has done so.*

Some websites will not work properly if pop-ups are blocked. If this happens, you can choose to allow pop-ups from the website.

16.4 Viruses, trojans and worms

Viruses, trojans and **worms** are little programs that install themselves on your computer without you knowing about it. This normally happens when you download something from the Internet or when you open an email. Like human viruses, a computer virus will infect your computer causing all sorts of problems. Some are worse than others. Really bad ones will delete everything on your computer.

Trojans are viruses that are hidden inside another file (as in Trojan Horse). Worms are viruses that are designed to infect lots of different files in your computer, making them difficult to get rid of.

What to do about it:

- ▶ *Only download from reputable sites or secure sites as explained in Chapter 15.*
- ▶ *Do not open emails (especially email attachments) if you do not know who they are from.*
- ▶ *Use anti-virus software. You can get free software from the Internet or you can buy it from companies such as McAfee or Norton.*
- ▶ *Keep your anti-virus software up-to-date as new viruses come out every day.*

- *Keep your version of Windows up-to-date as many updates contain fixes for well-known viruses.*

16.5 Spyware and adware

This is software that installs itself on your computer without you knowing about it. It can do this any time you are on the Internet. The software collects personal information that you fill in when online, and tracks which websites you visit. The information it gathers is usually used for marketing purposes.

What to do about it:

- *You can download free software from the Internet that will check your computer for spyware/adware, or you can buy software that will do it for you. This type of software is called* **Spyware** *or* **adware** *removal software.*
- *Keep your version of Windows up-to-date. Once you have bought Windows you are entitled to free updates from their website (www.microsoft.com).*

16.6 Creating a backup of your work

Most of these threats are relatively minor. The most dangerous of all these threats is that you get a virus.

Viruses vary in seriousness. For example, some viruses just do annoying things like automatically redirect you from one website to another, or maybe it will close down Internet Explorer automatically without warning.

In serious cases, viruses can destroy any of the information stored in your computer.

What to do about it:

▶ *Keep the original copies of all CDs/DVDs that came with any software that you bought, in a safe place.*

Hints and tips

If your computer came with Windows already on it, make sure that you ask your computer supplier for an original copy of the software on CD. This is proof that you have bought the software legally, and you can use it to set the computer up again if you get a bad virus.

Make a **backup** of anything that you have saved. The best way to do this is to copy it onto a CD or DVD. This will only work if your computer has a rewritable CD or DVD.

DVDs are more expensive to buy but can store much more data, so use DVDs if you can.

1 *Open the CD/DVD drawer on your computer by pressing the button.*

2 *Insert either a CD-R, CD-RW, DVD-R or DVD-RW shiny side down.*

3 *After a few seconds you may be asked what you want to do with the CD/DVD. If so, select the option to 'Burn files to disk'. If not, don't worry as you can open it shortly.*

4 *Click on 'Start'.*

5 *Click on 'Documents library'. This is where most of your files will be saved to. Notice that there are also libraries for music, photographs and videos. You can create a copy of all the information in the Documents library on a CD/DVD.*

6 *Press CTRL and A at the same time. You will see that all the files and folders are highlighted.*

7 *Point the mouse at any one of the files, right click and select 'Copy'.*

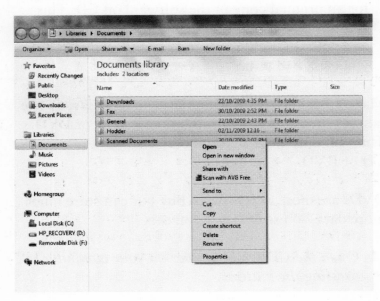

8 *On the left-hand side, click on the CD or DVD. In this case it is a DVD.*

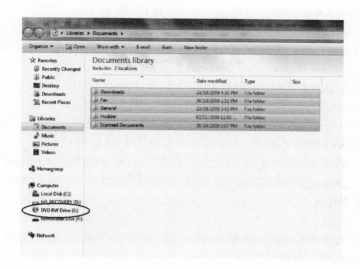

9 *You will be prompted to give your CD or DVD a name. Type in a suitable title, e.g. 'Documents backup April 2010'.*

10 *It will take a few seconds to format (prepare) the CD or DVD. A blank window is now displayed. This represents the contents of the CD or DVD, which is currently empty.*

11 *Right click anywhere in the white space.*

12 *Select 'Paste' from the list. The computer will now start copying all the files and folders in your Documents library ready to put them on the CD or DVD. This could take a while. You will get a progress bar that gives you an idea of how long this will take.*

Hints and tips

There is only so much information that you can physically store on the disk. If there is too much information you will get an error message at this point and you will have to go back to step 6 and choose individual files and folders within your Documents Library, instead of trying to do it all in one go.

13 *When it has finished, the CD/DVD will automatically eject. Label it – you can buy special pens for writing on CDs – and keep it somewhere safe.*

If you ever need to get the information back again from this CD/DVD:

1 *Put the disc in the drive.*
2 *Click on 'Start'.*
3 *Click on 'My Computer'.*
4 *Select the CD/DVD and copy files back from there to the folders that you want them in.*

IMPORTANT THINGS TO REMEMBER FROM THIS CHAPTER

1 When you are connected to the Internet there is a risk that the data on your computer could be damaged or stolen.

2 The overall threat is quite small. Some threats are nothing more than annoyances but you could lose everything that is stored on your computer.

3 Junk email or 'spam' is unsolicited email that turns up in your Inbox. Most of it is just trying to sell you something. Some of it could contain viruses.

4 You can avoid most of it by setting up spam filters. Don't open an email unless you know who it's from.

5 Pop-ups are annoying little windows that pop up when you are visiting websites. Usually they are just advertising something. Using a 'pop-up blocker' will get rid of most of them.

6 Viruses are little programs that install themselves on your computer and are designed to affect it in some way.

7 You should use anti-virus software and keep it up-to-date as new viruses come out all the time.

8 *Spyware and adware record what websites you visit and send the information back to companies that then use it for marketing purposes.*

9 *You can get software that will detect and delete these.*

10 *You should take regular backups of your work, and store these safely in a different location to your computer. Then if anything happens to your computer, at least you have all of your files.*

17

Arranging and booking your travels

In this chapter you will learn
- *how to find suitable travel websites*
- *how to book a holiday/flight*
- *how to check train times and buy tickets*
- *how to use a route-finder for UK road travel*

17.1 Introduction

In Chapter 9 we looked at the basic skills required to **surf** the Internet. Once you have got to grips with using a search engine (such as Google), you can use it to search for absolutely everything, including travel and holidays. The problem is if you just type 'holidays' into a search engine you will end up with millions of **hits** and it will be impossible to look through all of them.

One solution to this problem is to put more specific words into the search engine so that it only finds websites that are relevant to your requirements. Another solution to this problem is to find the web address of particular companies that you could use to arrange your travels. For example, Saga arrange holidays specifically for the over 50s, so you could do a search specifically for this company.

17.2 Searching for travel and holiday websites

1 *Open Internet Explorer.*
2 *Type www.google.co.uk into the address bar. The Google search engine will now load. You may prefer to use a different search engine to Google. These instructions will work for any.*
3 *The trick now is to make the key words as specific as possible. For example, to find some cheap airline tickets to Melbourne in Australia, in the search box, type '"cheap tickets" + Melbourne'. The use of speech marks means that it will only find websites with that exact phrase in it. The use of the + means that the website must also have the word Melbourne in it.*
4 *Click on the 'pages from the UK' button.*
5 *Click on 'Google search'. This search would bring up these results:*

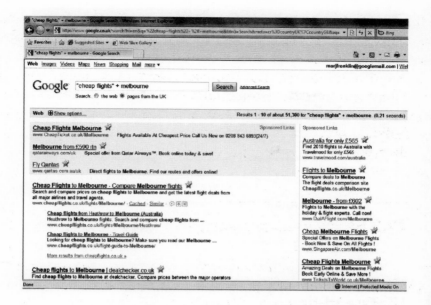

It has brought up 51,300 hits in this case, which is still too many to search through, but you should hopefully find what you are looking for within the first few pages of the results. Notice the first three results that have a pink background, and also note the results shown down the right-hand side of the page. These are all **sponsored links**, which means that the companies have paid Google to make sure that their websites appear on the first page.

You can now look at these results, read the text about each website and then decide which ones you want to look at. It is worth looking at a few different sites for comparison purposes.

> *To move onto the other pages, scroll to the bottom of the page and use the 'Next' button, or click on the page numbers.*

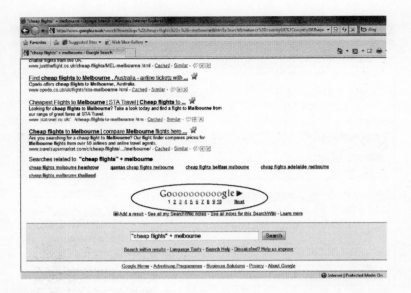

Hints and tips

If you know which company you want to use but you don't know their web address, then use the search engine to type in their name. It will then be displayed in the results page and you can link to it from there.

17.3 Choosing and booking a ticket/holiday

Once you have found the website you want to use, you then need to find the holiday or flight that you want, and book it. This process will be different depending on which company you use, as all of their websites are slightly different. However, the principle is the same in each case. You choose the holiday you want and then you have to fill in a form and make payment using your credit card.

We will use Saga Holidays as an example:

1 *Type www.saga.co.uk into the address bar of Internet Explorer. Their opening page will now be displayed.*

2 *Click on the links to their travel pages.*
3 *The different types of holidays are all shown and you can follow the links to find out more about individual types of holidays.*

Every company's web pages are different so you need to take a bit of time to look around the site and find what you want. In this example, we will work through the process of booking a short break in Paris.

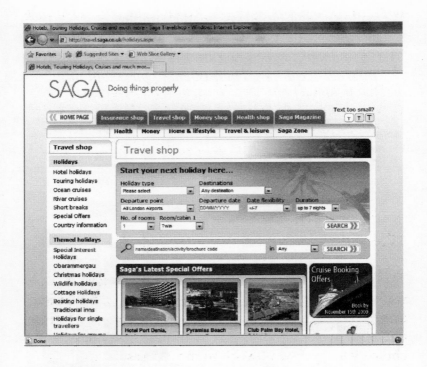

All holiday/flight booking sites use a search facility to check availability of whatever you are trying to book. You will be asked to type in your requirements in terms of dates, number of people travelling, etc. Saga has this search facility on this page under 'Start you holiday here...'

4 *Fill in your details and click in 'Search'. A page of results will be shown from which you choose the deal that you want. Again this may take some time as you might not want to book the first one it offers you.*

5 *When you have found the deal you want, all holiday/ travel websites will then take you through a few screens that you need to fill in. There will be a 'Next'*

or 'Proceed' button of some sort at the bottom of each
page showing you where to go next. You are asked for
lots of details including your credit card number.

6 When you have filled everything in, click on
the 'Process' button. You will then be given a
confirmation of your booking, which you can print
out as proof of purchase. Some websites will also
send you an email to confirm the details, and post
confirmation out to you as well.

17.4 Finding and booking train tickets

The process of finding and booking train tickets is
similar to booking a holiday, although it is a bit easier
as there are fewer options. In the UK, train routes are
operated by specific companies, so you don't have any
choice who you travel with in most cases.

There are two main websites that you can use to find
and book train tickets:

▶ _www.nationalrail.co.uk_
▶ _www.thetrainline.com_

Both work in a similar way, where you type in the route
that you want to take, and it will show you what trains
are available. You can then book them and pay for
them online.

1 Type _www.nationalrail.co.uk_ into the address bar
in Internet Explorer.

2 *Type in the details of the journey you want to take. This example shows a journey from London to Manchester.*

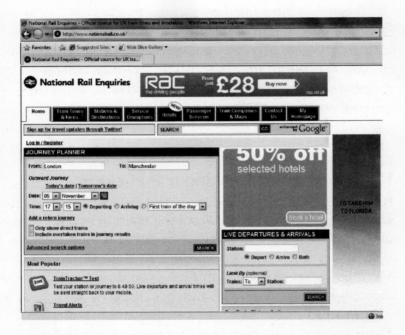

3 *Click on 'Search'. Like the holiday booking, you are now taken through several screens where you finalize the details of your journey, type in your personal details and payment details.*

4 *Complete all the details requested as you move through the screens.*

Hints and tips

All websites are different, but they are all designed to be easy to use. It should be clear how to move from one screen to the next. The link to the next page is usually at the bottom of the page.

17.5 Using a route-planner for a road journey

If you are planning a road trip, you can get detailed instructions and maps free on the Internet. All you have to do is type in the start point and your destination. A few websites offer this service. Two of the main ones are provided by motoring organizations:

▶ *www.theaa.com*
▶ *www.rac.co.uk*

Both have the route planner facility on their home page, which makes them very easy to find. In this example, we will use the RAC website.

1 *Type www.rac.co.uk.*

2 *The route planner is near the top of the page as shown. Type where you want to start your journey from and where you want to go to in the two boxes. This can be a place name or postcode. Then click 'Go'.*

3 *You may get another screen asking you to confirm the two destinations. Click 'Go' on screen. After a few seconds, a map will be displayed showing the route.*

4 *Scroll down the page and you will find detailed instructions on the route, including distances and approximate timings.*

5 *Click on the 'Route Map' tab to see a map of the route.*

6 *At the top of the instructions you have an option to print so you can take a paper copy with you on your journey.*

IMPORTANT THINGS TO REMEMBER FROM THIS CHAPTER

1 *You can arrange all type of transport and travel through the Internet, from holiday arrangements to local travel and traffic news and route planning.*

2 *Thousands of holiday companies use the Internet as their main marketing tool. This can produce some very competitive prices so shop around.*

3 *You can use a search engine to find suitable websites, or go to the websites of well-known holiday companies.*

4 *Most holiday websites work in a similar way in that you can search or browse for the holiday you want and then book and pay for it online.*

5 *Holiday websites are organized to make it easy to find what you want, e.g. searching by country, or date, or holiday type.*

6 *In many cases, all of the paperwork you need for your holiday is sent online and can be printed out prior to your departure.*

7 *Train travel can also be organized using websites in the same way as booking a holiday.*

8 *Train travel websites often offer much cheaper fares than buying at the station, particularly if you buy in advance.*

9 *Route-planning is available free on the Internet. The websites will give you step by step directions and a map, which you can print out.*

10 *Some websites that offer route-planning also have up-to-date traffic information to help with your planning.*

18

....

Banking online and other financial services

In this chapter you will learn
- *how to access your bank online*
- *how to run your current account*
- *how to carry out typical banking transactions*
- *how to access other financial services*
- *about price comparison sites*

18.1 Introduction

All of the main high street banks now offer an online banking service. It is possible to carry out most banking transactions online without having to visit your branch or use the telephone, including:

▶ *Checking your balance*
▶ *Viewing statements*
▶ *Paying bills*
▶ *Changing or cancelling standing orders and direct debits*
▶ *Transferring money*

You can also access a range of other financial services including arranging loans, mortgages, life insurance, ISAs and investments. You might want to do this through your existing bank, or you can use the Internet to shop around.

18.2 Getting started with online banking

Before you start online banking, you have to register your details with the bank for security purposes. Depending on the bank, you may need to do this over the phone or in the branch. Some banks allow you to do it using the Internet. If you want to do online banking with your existing bank, you will find details of how to register on their website.

Part of the registration process is to choose a security code (like a PIN) and answers to security questions (for example, mother's maiden name or first school). Once registered you will have to type in your sort code, account number and then you will be asked for the PIN and for the answer to the security question.

Hints and tips

All banks use slightly different security methods. Some ask for selected digits of the PIN, others ask you to choose dates as the security question.

Once registered, you can **log on** to your account. This example shows you the procedure for the Alliance and Leicester bank. The screens of other banks' websites will look different to this, but the basic processes will be the same regardless of the bank.

1 *Open 'Internet Explorer' and load the website of the bank. In this case, it is <u>www.alliance-leicester.co.uk</u>. This is the Alliance and Leicester log-on screen, which is typical of any bank's. It asks you for a Customer ID and security details.*

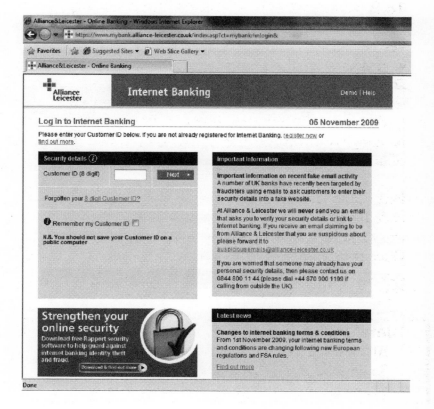

2 *Click in each box and type in the details.*
3 *Click on 'OK' to move on to the next screen.*

You will now be asked a series of security questions, which although annoying are very important in preventing fraud.

Once through the log-on screens, you will be shown your accounts. This view is of their current account. There is a list of options on the left-hand side, where you can carry out transactions such as paying bills and direct debits.

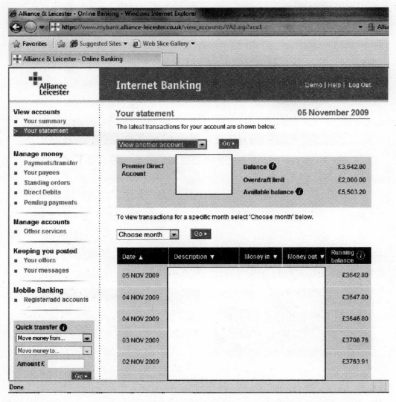

Note that for security reasons, we have blanked out some of the details on the screen images used in this chapter.

A list of recent transactions is shown in the table. This will include cheques, cash withdrawals, direct debits and standing orders. You can view a whole statement by finding and clicking on the link to 'Statements'. These are the electronic equivalent of the ones that you get through the post. Most banks will let you view statements from up to a year ago.

You can still ask the bank to send you paper copies of your statements, or you can print them out from here.

18.3 Carrying out transactions

As well as viewing your statements, you can pay bills, set up, change or cancel standing orders and direct debits and transfer money to other accounts. For example, to change or cancel a standing order:

1 *Find the link to 'Standing Orders'. In this case it is on the left-hand side of the screen. All of your existing standing orders will now be displayed.*
2 *To change or cancel a standing order, double click on the name of the person or organization who is receiving the money from you. The individual details of the standing order are now shown and you can amend or cancel it by clicking on the appropriate link.*

Once you are familiar with one transaction, all of the others are very similar. For example, managing your direct debits and bill payments is very similar to sorting out your standing orders.

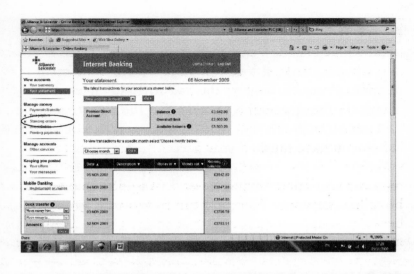

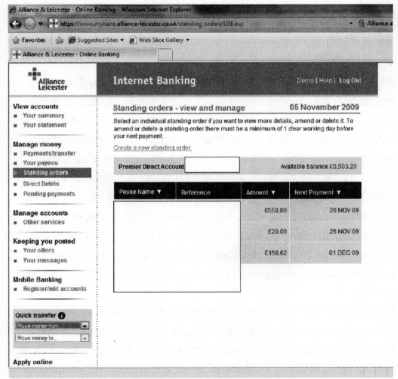

When you have finished banking, it is important that you log off from the website, rather than just clicking on the cross. There will be a link to 'log off' or it might be called 'sign out'. This guarantees that the connection between your computer and the bank's is closed, which makes you safe from hackers.

18.4 Other financial services

The Internet has become an important factor for all financial services businesses. In addition to the banks, there are lots of other financial services available over the Internet including loans, insurance, investments, mortgages and pensions. All the big companies now have websites as well as their high street presence.

Many financial services businesses offer cheaper deals if you buy online, because it saves them money. For example, if you buy car insurance online, many companies will offer you a 10 per cent discount.

Choosing which of these businesses to use involves the same decision-making process that you would use if you bought from them without doing it online. For example, you might choose to use a company because they are the cheapest, or because they offer the best service, or because you trust them. You should apply the same criteria when choosing whom to deal with online.

To access the websites of these businesses you either need to know the web address, which you can type straight into Internet Explorer, or you can use a search engine to find them.

18.5 Price comparison sites and money search engines

A relatively new phenomenon on the Internet is the price comparison site. These are websites that are set up to collate information about all sorts of products and services (including financial services) from lots of different companies and then compare them. The idea is that they do the shopping around for you, so that you only need to use one website. They collate information from most *but not all* of the major companies in the UK.

There are also websites that call themselves 'money search engines'. These are like normal search engines (e.g. Google) but the results are focused on financial topics.

There are lots to choose from. Some popular ones at the moment are:

- ▶ *www.moneysupermarket.com*
- ▶ *www.comparethemarket.com*

- *www.confused.com*
- *www.kelkoo.co.uk*
- *www.pricerunner.co.uk*

This is not an exhaustive list and if you type 'price comparison site + finance' into a search engine, you will find others to choose from.

They all work in the same basic way. For example, using comparethemarket.com:

1 *Type www.comparethemarket.com into the address bar of Internet Explorer.*
2 *Notice there are tabs showing the different aspects that the website can do comparisons on.*

You can now click on the links to look at certain types of financial services, e.g. Loans, Credit Cards, etc., or you can use the search facility. Many websites have their own search facilities, which you can use to search for something just on their website.

To use a search facility:

3 *Type the search words into the search box and click on 'Search'. In this example taken from Kelkoo, the site will be searched for details on ISAs.*

You can look through the results like you would with any search engine results. There is a small amount of text about each ISA and a link to the website of the company who are offering it. There are also some sponsored links at the top. Once you have linked to the website, you will be able to buy financial services online in the same way that you can buy anything else online.

Another example is www.moneysupermarket.com.

4 *Type www.moneysupermarket.co.uk into the address bar of Internet Explorer. You can see that their site is organized slightly differently and looks different, but basically it does the same thing as Kelkoo. In this example, we will compare the cost of personal loans.*
5 *Click on 'Money'.*

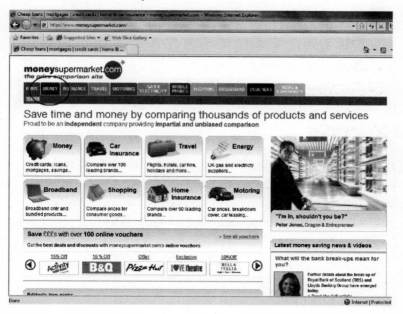

6 *Click on 'Compare Loans'. You can now type in the amount you want to borrow and it will compare the cost of borrowing from several different companies, and then provide you with a ranked list of results like the one shown here.*

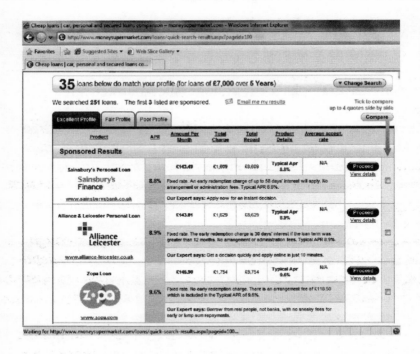

Again, think of this like the list of results that you get from a search engine. You can scroll through them, and click on them to go to the website of the company offering the loan. You can then apply online, or phone them up, or enter your details and they will call you back.

IMPORTANT THINGS TO REMEMBER FROM THIS CHAPTER

1 *Almost all of the main high street banks now offer an online banking service.*

2 *You can do almost all of the same things online that you can with a high street bank.*

3 *To set up online banking you have to go through a registration process, which is a bit more in-depth than usual. This is because the banks have to ensure that their websites are safe from fraudsters.*

4 *Once registered you can view your account online, looking at individual payments in and out of your accounts.*

5 *Statements are available online although you can usually only view the last few months' worth. You can print paper copies if you want to.*

6 *You can also view and set up direct debits, standing orders and transfers.*

7 *A range of other financial services are available online, for example, mortgages, loans and insurance. It is possible to get discounts as it reduces the companies' overheads to do it online.*

8 *You can use a search engine to find the websites of different financial services companies and compare the deals on offer.*

9 *Comparison websites can be a useful way of finding a good deal but not all financial service providers are listed on these sites.*

10 *Comparison websites are set up to allow you to compare deals on a like-for-like basis.*

19

Buying from an online auction

In this chapter you will learn
- *how to use the eBay auction site*
- *how to find items you want*
- *how to bid*
- *how to pay for your purchases*

19.1 Introduction

eBay is currently the world's biggest online auction site boasting more than 230 million users worldwide with millions of items for sale at any one time.

It works much in the same way as a traditional auction in that items are offered for sale, you look at them and read the description, and then decide whether you want to bid on the item or not. Many other people will be doing the same thing and bidding against you. The big difference with a real auction is the period of time over which the bidding takes place, as it can be several days. At the end of this period, if your bid is the highest, you win. You then pay for the product and the seller sends it to you, or you go and pick it up.

Although eBay was originally intended for items of relatively low value, it is now possible to buy virtually anything on eBay including cars, holidays and even houses.

19.2 Getting started

First, you need to register. To do this, you must already have an email address. If you do not have one, refer to Chapter 5.

1 *Open Internet Explorer® either from the desktop, from the Windows Taskbar or from the 'Start' menu.*
2 *In the address bar, type www.ebay.co.uk. (eBay operates in more than 30 countries, so make sure that you use the correct version for the country that you are in.) The opening page is displayed and will look something like this.*
3 *Click on the 'Register' button. You will be asked for your personal details and email contact details. You will also be asked to think of a user ID and password, which you will need to use every time you log on to eBay.*
4 *Complete the form. This may take a few minutes.*
5 *Make a note of your user ID and remember your password.*

6 *When you have completed the form, you will be sent an email from eBay. This is an automatic process and should be instant.*

7 *Go to your email account and open the email from eBay.*

8 *In the email, you are asked to click on a link that will activate your eBay account. Click on the link. It will take you back to the eBay website where you can now start bidding for products.*

9 *To make sure you are in the 'Buy' section, click on the link to 'Buy' in the top right-hand corner of the page:*

19.3 Finding what you want

There are two ways to find the items you are looking for:

▶ *You can browse, which means you can look*
through a wide range of products under certain
categories.
▶ *You can search, which means you type in a few*
keywords that describe the item you want and it
will search through all the items and display only
those items that match the description you have
typed in.

BROWSING FOR AN ITEM

If you do not specifically know what you want, then
browsing through the eBay categories is the best option.

For example, if you want to look at antique chairs, but do not have a specific item in mind:

1 *Look through the categories until you find the one you want. In this case, it will be under 'Antiques' so click on this link. You are now presented with a more detailed list of categories within the Antiques section.*

2 *Under Antique Furniture click on 'Chairs'.*

3 *You are now at the screen that lists all of the items that are for sale under this category. In this example, there are 3048 items for sale. To view the entire list of items for sale, you need to scroll down. It is not possible to show all 3048 items on one page, so at the bottom of the first page, there are links to several other pages.*

On the left-hand side of each page, you will see that there are further subcategories for the type, age or style of the chair. For example, there are categories for 'Dining Chairs', 'Armchairs', etc. This will help you to narrow down your search, reducing the number of items listed.

Hints and tips

It would take you hours to view all 3048 items in this example so it would be better to try to narrow down the search if you can, using the subcategories.

SEARCHING FOR AN ITEM

The preferred method of finding what you want on eBay is to type in a few keywords that describe it. As you saw in the previous section, browsing through categories can be time-consuming as there are often so many items for sale.

1 *Click on the 'Buy' button again to take you back to the main buying page where all the categories are listed.*
2 *At the top of this page, there is a 'Search' box. This example will show you how to search for a specific item, a garden hammock. Click in the 'Search' box and type 'garden hammock'.*
3 *You can narrow down the search by searching only within a category using the box to the right of the search box. In the 'In this category' box, which currently reads 'All categories', select 'Home & Garden'. If you do not know which category something fits in to, you can just leave this box set to 'All categories'.*
4 *Click on 'Search'.*

After a few seconds, you will be presented with a list of all the garden hammocks that are currently for sale.

19.4 Selecting your item

Once you have located an item that you are interested in, you need to get a few more details about it and the seller. In the first instance you need to know the price, how many bids there are on it, and how long there is left on the auction.

The screen listing all of the items gives you some useful information to help you decide whether to look in more detail at the item.

These are:

- **Photograph of the product** – *the seller puts this on. If there isn't a photograph, be suspicious.*
- **Item Title** – *a brief description put on by the seller.*
- **Bids** – *shows you the number of people who have put in a bid on this item. If it is displaying the 'Buy It Now' symbol it means that it you must pay the price quoted, you cannot bid for it. Other option in here are 'Buy it Now or Best Offer', which means they are open to offers and 'Classified', which means it is an advert like the ones you get in the back of your local paper.*
- **Price** – *the highest price currently bid or the asking price if it is a 'Buy it now' item.*
- **Postage** – *how much the seller will charge you to send the item. Keep an eye out for over-the-top charges.*
- **Time Left** – *how many days or hours there are left until the auction closes. When the auction closes, the highest bidder at that point wins.*

This information is displayed for every item that is for sale. If you are still interested in the item you can now find out more about it and the seller.

19.5 Finding out more about the items and the seller

To view more details about any specific item:

1 *Click on the photograph or on the item title. This then displays a further page that gives you details about the product, usually some more photographs and the seller rating, which gives you an idea of how reliable the seller is.*

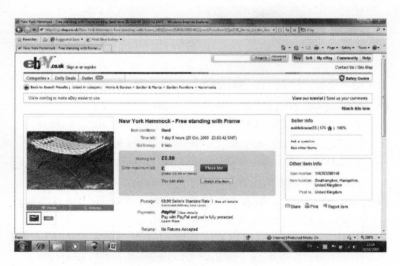

2 *A fuller description of the product can be obtained by scrolling down the page.*

On the right-hand side is a seller rating. When people buy items from eBay™ they are asked to rate the seller and make comments about them. You can view these comments and read the ratings by following these links. It will show you the number of people who have commented and provide an overall rating. In this example, the seller has 575 ratings and they are all positive giving a 100 per cent rating.

You can contact the seller directly to ask about the product or delivery arrangements, etc. This is advisable on larger value items in particular.

Hints and tips

eBay provides useful hints and tips about trading on their website. For example, this page in the diagram above has a link to a section on safe buying tips.

19.6 Making a bid

Once you have found the item you want, you can bid on it. If either of the 'Buy It Now' options or 'Classified Ad' logos are shown, you can just buy it at this point without having to bid at all or contact the seller with an offer. Assuming that bidding is required:

1 *From the current screen, click on the 'Place Bid' button.*

2 *This will take you to a screen where you can type in how much you want to bid.*

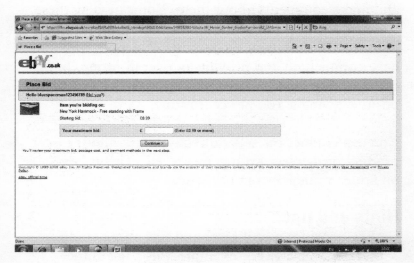

3 *A useful feature here is that you can type in the maximum amount you are prepared to pay and eBay will automatically keep increasing your bid, if you are out-bid by someone else. If the price goes beyond your maximum bid, it will stop bidding and you will not win the auction.*

4 *Finally, you are asked to confirm the bid. It is at this point that you are entering a legal contract to buy the item. So if you win, you must buy it. Only click on continue if you want to buy the item!*

5 *The next step is to keep an eye on the bidding from time to time, or just wait until the time runs out and see whether you have won.*

6 *eBay has a feature called 'My eBay'. You can opt to 'Watch this item', which means that it will put the item you are interested in into a list for you, where you can watch the progress of the bidding.*

To do this, from the item's description screen like the one shown, click on 'Watch this item'.

7 *To view the 'My eBay' area, click on 'My eBay' near the top of the window. The My eBay screen looks like the following illustration. The hammock is listed here and it is possible to view the bidding as it progresses.*

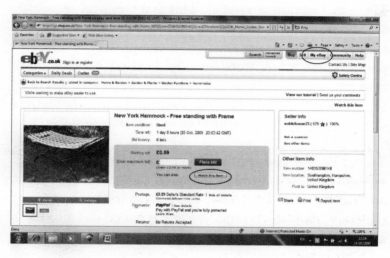

19.7 Winning and paying

When you win an auction for an item or if you opt to 'Buy It Now' you need to pay for the item. If you win or lose an auction, you will be informed by email. There are different ways of paying. You are supplied with contact details of the seller. This is often just an email address or maybe a phone number. If this is the case, you could just contact the seller and make arrangements like any other buying/selling arrangement.

Alternatively, you can do it all online or via the post with no need for any contact at all. Many sellers accept cheques but will require you to post the cheque and allow time for it to clear. This is where the seller rating is important, as you need to be confident that you will receive the item.

The other option is PayPal. This is a free and secure service where you pay using your credit or debit card via email. This is quicker than a cheque as the money will transfer much more quickly. It also provides protection in the eventuality that the item is not sent, or you want to reclaim your money because the item is significantly different from the way it was described.

To use PayPal you will need to register with the PayPal website first. This process is similar to registering for eBay and can be done by following the links to PayPal from the eBay site or by typing 'www.paypal.co.uk' into the address bar and then clicking on the 'Sign Up Now' link.

Once you have done this you will be able to use this method wherever the seller accepts PayPal. You will receive an email confirming your order, and you click on the 'Pay Now' option.

19.8 Things to watch out for when using eBay

In common with anything else on the Internet, there are plenty of dodgy people out there who might try to rip you off. The anonymous nature of the Internet perhaps makes this a bit easier for these people. The best advice is to use the seller ratings to make a judgement about how reliable someone might be.

Decide how much you want to spend and stick to it. In common with traditional auctions, it can be tempting to keep upping the price that you are willing to pay, only to regret it later. Many bidders leave it until the last minute to make their bids; so don't get caught up in a bidding war.

Make sure you are aware of all the charges that will be added. Keep an eye on postage costs and VAT. Many businesses now use eBay as their main way of selling products, and they will have to add on VAT. Also, make sure that the item is for sale in your country, or you may have to pay additional shipping costs and tax.

Finally, eBay has become an international phenomenon and as a result, there is a lot of information written about it. A good starting point is the company's own Help centre, which can be accessed by clicking the 'Help' tab on their home page.

IMPORTANT THINGS TO REMEMBER FROM THIS CHAPTER

1 *eBay is an Internet-based auction website where you can buy and sell almost anything from small second-hand items to cars and even houses.*

2 *You need to register with eBay in order to buy or sell. You can also register for PayPal, which is a secure online electronic payment system.*

3 *You can either browse by category to find what you want, or use the search facility.*

4 *There is a lot of information available about the item you want to buy and the person or online business who is selling it.*

5 *You can make a bid on an item and then continue to bid as the price changes. Alternatively, you can place a maximum bid.*

6 *Some items are available to buy straight away or shown as a classified ads, which means you do not have to bid as such, just make an offer.*

7 *There is a 'watch this item' feature which allows you to keep an eye on particular items whether you are bidding on them or not.*

8 *If you win the auction you will be notified and you then have to make payment, which may be via PayPal or more traditional methods.*

9 *As with any purchase, you need to satisfy yourself that you are happy with the item and the person selling it before you start bidding.*

10 *eBay has become a worldwide phenomenon with many businesses now using it to make a living.*

20

....

Selling at an online auction

In this chapter you will learn
- *how to add a listing to sell an item on eBay*
- *how to categorize and describe your item*
- *how to add a photograph*
- *how to register as an eBay seller*

20.1 Getting started

1 *Open Internet Explorer either from the desktop or from the 'Start' icon.*
2 *In the address bar, type www.ebay.co.uk.*
3 *The opening page is displayed. In the previous chapter you registered yourself with the eBay site, which you only have to do once. From now on when you use eBay, you just sign in.*
4 *Type in your user name and password and click on 'Sign in'.*

20.2 Setting up the listing for your item

1 *At the main eBay page, click on 'Sell' at the top of the screen and you will be prompted for some details on the item that you are selling.*

2 *Type a description of the item into the 'What are you selling' box, e.g. 'Gent's bicycle', and then click on the 'Start selling' button.*

3 *You are now on a screen that has all the stages you need to go through to set up your auction. Notice that it is colour-coded to make it easy to see which stage you are at.*

4 *The next stage is to select a category under which your item will appear on the site. eBay will suggest suitable categories. Click on the one that is most*

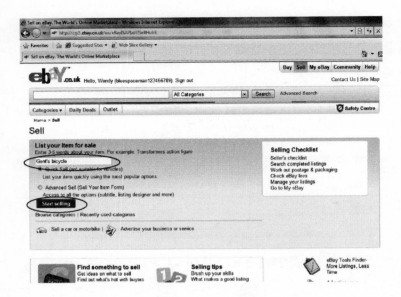

appropriate. In the case of a bicycle this will be
'Cycling – Bikes'. You can place your item in more
than one category if you think it is appropriate.

5 Scroll down so that you can complete the next stage
which is to add a photograph by clicking on the
'Add photo' button. Buyers are more likely to show
an interest in listings that include photographs. If
there is no photograph they might be suspicious
about the condition of what you are selling.

6 Browse your computer to find the image, which
is probably in your Pictures library. This chapter
assumes that you have a photo of the item on your
computer and that you know its file name and
which folder it is in.

7 The next stage is to type a more detailed description
of the item.

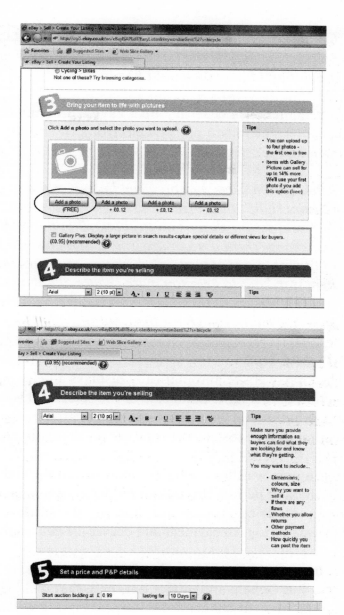

8 *Continue through the stages completing the details on price, including the reserve price (least you will accept) and how you would like to be paid.*

> You might consider setting up a PayPal account as this allows people to pay you electronically. It is quick and secure.

9 *Click on the 'Save and preview' button at the bottom right of the screen.*
10 *The next screen allows you to check all of the details and change them if necessary. It will also give you lots of other options of ways in which you can make your item stand out to give you more chance of selling it for a higher price. These cost more money, so it's up to you whether you go for these options or not.*

Hints and tips

The eBay website automatically displays a help section on the right-hand side of the screen. This is really useful and gives hints and tips related to the section of the website that you are on at the time.

You can now wait for the bids to come in. At the end of the auction period, the highest bidder wins (assuming your reserve price has been met) and you then make arrangements to take payment and deliver the item to them.

eBay has become an international phenomenon and there is lots of help and advice out there that will help you improve your chances of selling. There are whole books and websites dedicated to it. Some people have even become 'eBay millionaires' by using eBay as a way of selling. The eBay help screens are a useful start point, and you could use the web searching skills you have learnt in previous chapters to surf the Internet for more help and guidance.

20.3 Managing your account

You will be prompted to set up an account if you have not done so already. This is because eBay charges you fees for using their service so they need your bank details to collect the money. This is very similar to any other type of transaction that you might carry out on the Internet. You will be prompted for your personal details and bank account details.

1 *To manage your account at any time, click on 'My eBay' near the top right-hand side of the page.*
2 *Click on the 'Account' tab as shown:*

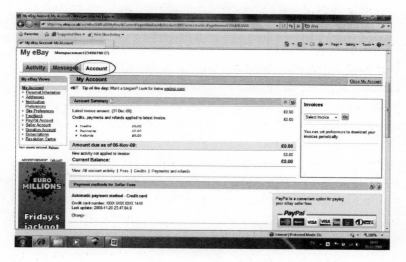

From here you can view all of your transactions include money made from selling on eBay and payments made. Notice that your payment details are near the bottom and you can change these at any time, for example, to link the account to a different bank account.

IMPORTANT THINGS TO REMEMBER FROM THIS CHAPTER

1 *You can use eBay to buy and sell items. You will need to register to do either.*

2 *When selling items, you need to complete a series of online forms completing details about your item(s) and yourself.*

3 *You must select a suitable category under which your item will be listed.*

4 *Add at least one photograph of your item. You have to pay more to show more photos, but it may be worth it if it increases interest in your item.*

5 *Bear in mind that you may be competing with lots of similar items, so you need to give people enough information to make them interested in yours.*

6 *You are prompted to indicate the lowest price (reserve) that you are willing to accept on the offer.*

7 *You are prompted to indicate how long you want the auction to run, which may be a matter of weeks, days or hours.*

8 *You can use eBay to sell items using either a 'buy it now' option or a classified advert. These do not go through the auction.*

9 *You need to think about what payment options you will accept. Most eBayers now use the PayPal facility.*

10 *You will have to provide financial information to eBay as it makes a charge for every item sold through its website.*

21

Doing your grocery shopping

In this chapter you will learn
- *how to check who delivers in your area*
- *how to register for online shopping*
- *how to find and select the products you want to buy*
- *how to book a delivery slot*
- *how to pay*

21.1 Introduction

Many, but not all of the big grocery retailers now offer an online shopping service. There are also lots of smaller, local shops that offer a home delivery service. The first stage of the process is to check that the retailer you want to use does deliver to your area. For example, Tesco, Sainsbury's, Asda and Waitrose all offer delivery services, but you do have to check that they will deliver in your locality. You also need to consider the cost of delivery, which is usually around £5. You can then order your products by filling up a **virtual** basket or trolley. You book your delivery slot, pay online and then wait for the van. Generally speaking you need to book a day or two in advance and then wait in for a delivery slot, which is normally given within a two-hour time period, e.g. 9 am–11 am.

The first time you shop online it might take quite a while, but it will be quicker when you do it subsequent times, because the websites use the 'favourites' idea that we looked at in Chapter 10, to remember the things that you bought last time.

21.2 Choosing an online grocery store

If you are lucky, you might have a choice of grocery shops where you live, and they might all offer online shopping. In other areas you might find that there is only one option. To check, you will need to go to the websites of the shops and type in your postcode.
To find the web address of the grocery shops you can either use a search engine, or you can type the address straight in to the address bar.

Hints and tips
The website addresses of big companies are usually quite predictable e.g. www.tesco.com, www.asda.com, www.waitrose.co.uk and www.sainsburys.co.uk. Even if you get the .co.uk or .com wrong at the end it will still take you to their website.

As an example:

1 *Open 'Internet Explorer' and type www.asda.com into the address bar.*

2 *Click on the link to 'Start shopping', which on this site is in the top left-hand corner. The first thing it will do is ask you for your postcode so that it can check whether they deliver in your area.*
3 *Type in your postcode and press 'Check postcode'. It will check instantly and give you a message indicating whether you can shop or not. If you can, you can proceed with the shopping. If not, you will have to try another shop.*

21.3 Registering for online shopping

The next step is to register your details by clicking on the 'Register now' link. In common with most websites, you will normally use your email address as your **user name** and then be asked to select a **password**. You will be asked for these two bits of information every time you want to **log on** to their site.

To register, you have to fill in a form with all of your personal details. Obviously, they will need your home address and phone number as they are delivering to your house, and your credit/debit cards details so that

you can make payment. Once you have filled the form
in you are ready to shop.

This is the log-on screen for Asda:

21.4 Filling up your basket/trolley

This is the main web page on the Asda website where
you choose what you want to buy. The first time you
do your shopping you have to choose everything from
scratch.

▶ *You can either use the search box and type in what you are looking for or you can browse through the categories on the tabs as shown:*

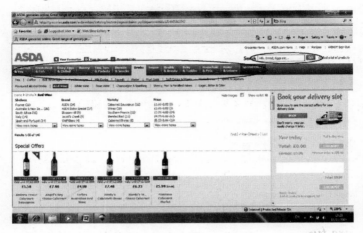

You will also notice that like real shops, you are bombarded with special offers, trying to entice you to add a few more items to your trolley. It's up to you whether you are enticed or not!

Once you have been through the whole process once you have an additional (quicker) option which is to use the 'Your favourites' option. This will show you the products you have purchased before.

Hints and tips

The 'browse' and 'search' options are a common feature of many websites, and they work in the same way on each site.

Once you have found the product you want, you add it to your trolley, and then move onto the next product.

When you have finished, you go to the 'Checkout', book your delivery slot and pay.

Let's work through three examples using each of the three methods:

BROWSING

In this example, we will buy a bottle of wine:

1 *Click on 'Drinks'.*
2 *There are further categories now displayed just below the tabs. Click on 'Red Wine'. All the red wines are now displayed, and you can scroll down and look through the list. You will notice that there are further categories allowing you to browse by country or price among other things.*

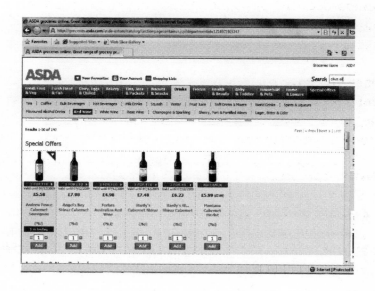

3 *When you have found the one you want, select how many bottles you want, and click on 'Add'. This is now added to your trolley and you can continue with your shopping. You can view the contents of your trolley at any time by clicking on the 'Your trolley' button on the right of the page. At the moment, it will just have one bottle of wine in it. Notice that you can see a running total of how much you have spent.*

SEARCHING

The 'search' option is much quicker than browsing, providing you know what you are looking for. You can be quite specific with your search words, e.g. if you want Asda own-brand olive oil then type in Asda olive oil to reduce the number of **hits**.

1 *Click in the 'Search' box and type': Olive oil'.*

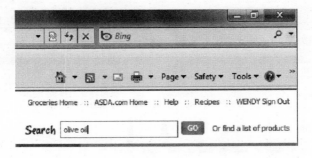

2 *Click on 'Go'. All the olive oils are now displayed, and you can scroll down and look through the list.*
3 *You add the product you want to your trolley in the same way as described before.*

FAVOURITES

If this is the first time you have shopped, you won't have any favourites yet, but it is shown here for future reference. Using favourites is probably the quickest way to shop, but you will have to do one shop first, so that it knows what your favourites are.

If you buy pretty much the same things every week, you can click on 'Shopping lists' and select last week's shopping order. You can then just go through and add and remove from this list. This is much quicker than building the list from scratch every week.

1 *Click on 'Favourites'. Everything that you have ever ordered is stored in your favourites. This means that you can look for it in your favourites rather than having to search the whole shop.*

2 *You can look at 'All favourites' which lists everything you have ever bought. Alternatively, you can look in particular categories, or select 'Shopping lists' which will show you your previous shopping lists.*

21.5 Booking a time slot and paying

Once you are happy that you have got everything you want, it's time to book your delivery slot and make payment.

1 *On the right-hand side, click on the link to 'Book your delivery slot'.*

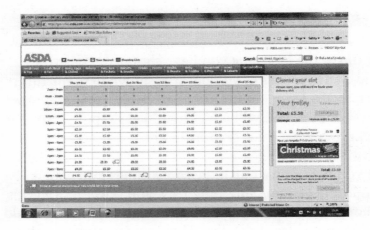

2 *Find the delivery slot you want, and click on it. Notice that some times are more popular than others and will already have been taken. Also the more popular times tend to cost more.*

3 *Go back to 'Your trolley'.*

4 *Click on 'Checkout'. At the checkout you can redeem any money-off vouchers by clicking on the link. If you have any vouchers they will have a code on them, which you have to type in at this point.*

5 *Most of the details on this page are already complete as they are taken from the information you gave when you registered. You can check and change them from here if you need to. For example, your credit/debit card number is shown here, so make sure that this is up to date. If you suddenly remember something else you need to buy, you can go back to the basket from here to add items.*

6 *Scroll to the bottom of this page and click 'Confirm order'.*

7 *You can now print out your order if you want to so that you have the list to check off the items when they are delivered.*

21.6 Taking delivery

All shops operate their deliveries in time slots, so it is important that you are able to stay in for the duration of that period. When the groceries arrive, if there are any products that were not available in the shop, they will substitute it for something similar. The delivery driver will tell you about these and they will be listed on his/her copy of your order. You don't have to accept the substitutions if you don't want them.

They will hand you their copy of your order with the final price on it. It may vary slightly from the price you were originally given because the substitutions may be have been a different price. They will then give you their hand-held computer device, and you sign on the screen to confirm receipt. Job done.

IMPORTANT THINGS TO REMEMBER FROM THIS CHAPTER

1 *Most of the major grocery retailers and lots of smaller local companies now offer an online shopping service.*

2 *For a charge of around £5, the store will do your shopping and deliver it to your door within a predefined two-hour time slot.*

3 *Ask around among family and friends to find out who delivers in your area and whether they are any good.*

4 *You can use the stores own websites to find out if they deliver in your area by typing in your postcode.*

5 *You have to register with the website, which will involve giving them your bank account details so that you can complete online transactions.*

6 *Most websites work by having an online basket or trolley, which you fill up with items and then take to the checkout – just like a real store.*

7 *You can browse by category or use a search facility on the website to find the items you want.*

8 *The website will allow you to store your favourites and will record previous shopping trips making it easy for you to do your shopping.*

9 *There are special offers on the website like you would find in store and you can also redeem vouchers.*

10 *When the goods are delivered, they will offer substitutes for anything that was not available in the store. You can reject those that are not satisfactory.*

22

Working and learning

In this chapter you will learn
- *how to find help and guidance on employment and pension issues*
- *how to find a new job*
- *how to find advice and information on starting your own business*
- *how to find voluntary work*
- *how to find training courses*

22.1 Introduction

Patterns of employment are constantly changing. It's hard to find a job for life these days, and the idea that you are on the scrapheap when you get over 50 is outdated. Many businesses value the experience that more mature employees bring to their work. It is also easier then ever to start your own business and capitalize on all that experience for yourself.

Patterns of education have changed too, with more and more older people taking part in courses, either for pleasure, or to get qualifications. For example, recent research by Age Concern suggests that over half of the 60–69-olds in the UK are taking part in some form of education.

There is a mass of information available on the Internet, and this chapter will point you in the direction of some of the most useful websites. The **web address** is given for every site mentioned, so all you have to do is type this address into the address bar in Internet Explorer.

22.2 Help on employment and pension issues

Older workers face some issues specifically related to their age. For example, there have been recent changes to the legislation on age discrimination. One very useful site provided by the government is <u>www.direct.gov.uk</u>.

This is a really useful site for all kinds of government information, not just employment. To find the employment information, follow the link to 'Employment'. You can now follow the various links depending on what you are interested in, e.g. 'Looking for work' or 'Resigning and retiring'.

More specific advice about pensions can be found at: www.thepensionservice.gov.uk

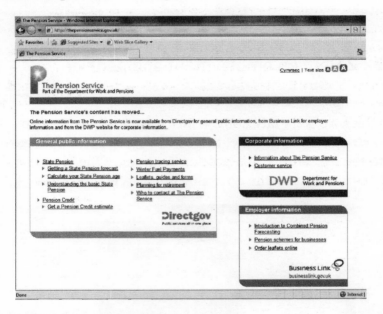

Hints and tips

Note that these site have .gov at the end of the address. This means that the site has been created by a department of the UK government.

Another government site that covers other aspects of finding work is at www.jobcentreplus.gov.uk. This has links to the New Deal 50 Plus service for those looking for work.

Another good source of information locally is your local government and county council websites. The easiest way to find your local one is to use a search engine and type in, for example: 'County Council + Leicestershire'. This should bring your council's website to the top of the list. You can then follow the links to local employment information.

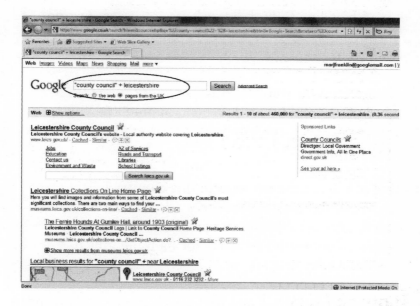

There is an 'Age Positive' campaign at www.agepositive. gov.uk, which provides lots of information and links for older workers. This site focuses on the particular benefits of employing older workers, and the experience and skills that they offer, as well as providing information on age discrimination, pensions and other issues.

22.3 How to find a job

If you are looking for work, there are thousands of jobs advertised on the Internet every day. There are so many online job websites now that it is difficult to know which one to choose. As ever, you could start by using a search engine to find the websites on offer. Typing 'Jobs' will bring back millions of hits, so you might want to be more specific with your search words.

Most of the job websites offer a facility to search for jobs by type and by area. When you find one you are interested in you can apply for it and send your CV online.

One of the biggest job sites in this country is www.monster.co.uk. The site works like a search engine, listing jobs that match your search words. In this example, the search is for banking jobs in Leicestershire.

The results are also listed like search engine results and you can work your way through them, clicking on the links to find out more about each job.

The jobs will have a link where you can apply online. To do this you will need to register with the website,

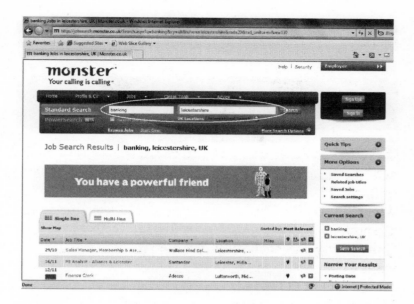

completing all your personal details. This site also has a facility to complete a detailed CV.

22.4 Starting your own business

As you get older you are more likely to want to start and run your own business. Around 25 per cent of people aged over 56 are self-employed. There is a lot of help and guidance available in the Internet.

Some of the sites we have looked at already feature sections on self-employment, e.g. www.direct.gov.uk. Further help can be found at www.businesslink.gov.uk.

Follow the links to 'Starting up'.

The Citizens Advice Bureau also has lots of useful information and links for the self-employed at http://www.adviceguide.org.uk/. Follow the links on the left-hand side to 'Employment' and then the 'Self-employment checklist'.

Notice that this site is useful for lots of other information too, not just about employment.

22.5 Volunteering

If you want to volunteer, there are a number of useful sites that will give you further information, and enable you to offer your services.

Go to www.volunteeringengland.org.uk. Click on 'I want volunteer'. You can then look for volunteering opportunities in your area.

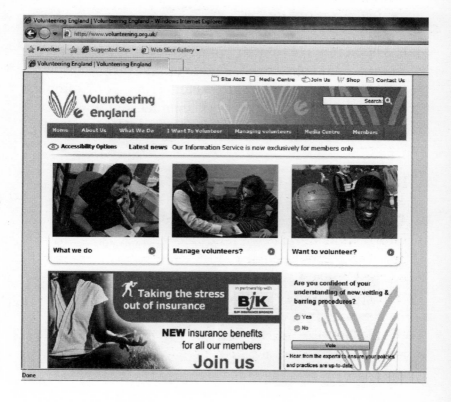

Other volunteering websites can be found at:

▶ *www.do-it.org.uk*
▶ *www.timebank.org.uk*
▶ *www.csv.org.uk*
▶ *www.vso.org.uk*

If you would like to offer your service to a particular charity, then use a search engine to find their website and then follow the links to volunteering. For example, the National Trust encourages volunteers at www. nationaltrust.org.uk. Follow the link to 'Get involved'.

22.6 Training and education

There are two main ways of using the Internet here. You can use it to search for courses that are running in your local area, or you can take an online course.

There are so many courses available throughout the country that it can be difficult to find the one you want. The government has a commitment to ongoing education and they will fund free places on courses for older people. These courses are run through the Adult Education departments of the local councils. Therefore, a good place to start is your local council website.

For example, to find all the courses running in Devon you would type 'county council + adult education + Devon'. This is a very specific search and should bring exactly what you want to the top of the list:

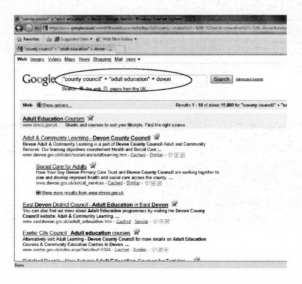

Once you have linked to the site, you can look for further links to the colleges and they will list the courses that are available. Some sites will have a search facility to make this quicker.

You may find links to free courses in some of the other websites we have mentioned in this chapter already, e.g. the over 50s section of the direct.gov.uk site.

You can also take **online courses** over the Internet. These are the modern version of what used to be called correspondence courses, where you may never actually meet your tutor, or fellow students. You carry out research and complete assignments and then send them over the Internet to your tutor to be marked.

You will communicate with your tutor using email and sometimes you may have an online conversation using the techniques explained in Chapter 12. Some courses do have a residential aspect where you all meet up somewhere, usually during the summer. You can do courses like this purely for pleasure, or it is possible to study to academic levels using this method.

The first task is to find an online college. Again, you can use the Internet to search for one. Some of the better known ones are:

- *www.bbc.co.uk/learning/onlinecourses/*
- *www.open.ac.uk*
- *www.learndirect.co.uk*

Notice that some of the websites end in .ac. This means that they are an academic institution, i.e. a university or college.

Many of the main universities now also offer online versions of their courses.

IMPORTANT THINGS TO REMEMBER FROM THIS CHAPTER

1 *There are now over 20 million over 50s in the UK, many of whom are taking part in either employment or education of some sort.*

2 *The Internet is a good way of keeping up-to-date with the changing world of employment and education.*

3 *The website www.direct.gov.uk contains masses of information relating to government services including advice on state pensions.*

4 *There are thousands of websites dedicated to people who are looking for work and these can be found using a search engine.*

5 *Local councils and job centres also have websites advertising jobs.*

6 *You can register with jobs websites and they will email you updates. You can also upload you CV to their sites for potential employers to see.*

7 *If you are thinking of starting your own business there is a lot of information and advice available.*

8 *You can use the Internet to find out about local, national and international volunteering opportunities.*

9 *You can use the Internet to find out about courses and night classes being offered around the country.*

10 *You can use the Internet to take an online course, a bit like a traditional 'correspondence course' but all done via websites and email.*

Accessing TV, radio and games

In this chapter you will learn
- *how to find radio, TV and games websites*
- *how to listen to live radio*
- *how to use listen-again services for radio programmes*
- *how to watch TV programmes*
- *how to play online games*

23.1 Introduction

Multimedia (the mixture of text, sounds and images) is what the Internet is all about. The Internet lets us access multimedia content (music, videos, games, etc.) whenever we want it. There are two main ways of doing this. The first, which is covered in this chapter, is going onto websites where we can watch TV, listen to radio and play games. The second, which is covered in the next chapter is downloading music and video to your computer so that you can view and listen to it without having to be online.

You do need to exercise a bit of caution with the websites that you use. The law of copyright covers music, film and computer games, among other things. The website that is providing these things must have permission to do so. Many sites are legal and do have permission to do this, and this chapter will show you some of these. Most websites have links to pages that explain the legal issues, and you should check that the sites you are using are legal.

Hints and tips

There is a big debate at the moment about copyright material and how it applies to the Internet. At the moment you can be sued for downloading material without the permission of the copyright holder.

23.2 Listening to the radio

There are two main ways of doing this. The first is that you can listen to live radio as it is being broadcast. The other is that you can use the 'listen-again' feature to listen to programmes that you missed the first time round.

There are hundreds of online radio stations and a quick search with a search engine will give you plenty to choose from. The beauty of the Internet is the range of different stations you can get access to. For example, you will find radio stations that cover very specific musical tastes. Some of these radio stations are free, and some are paid for.

Digital stations can be accessed through the Internet, or through digital TV, or through a DAB radio, but you cannot get digital radio stations on a normal radio.

We will look at the BBC stations, as they are provided free. There is a good selection of stations to choose from. There are 12 main stations that you can listen to, shown as different coloured tabs across the screen, plus you have access to all of the local radio stations as well, even if you are not in the area normally served by that station. Some of these stations are available on your normal radio, but some are only available as digital channels.

1 *Type www.bbc.co.uk/radio into the address bar of Internet Explorer.*

2 *If you know what station you want to listen to click on the link to the station. In this example we will go to Five Live.*

3 *From this page you can either listen live, which means you can hear what is being broadcast right now, or you can listen again to a programme that you missed.*

4 *To listen live, click on the 'Listen live' link.*

5 *The BBC website has its own media player called iPlayer, which it used for audio and video. iPlayer open in a new window and you should hear the broadcast coming out of your speakers.*

6 *To listen to a programme that has already been aired, you need to click on the 'Listen again' feature. All the programmes that are available are listed, and*

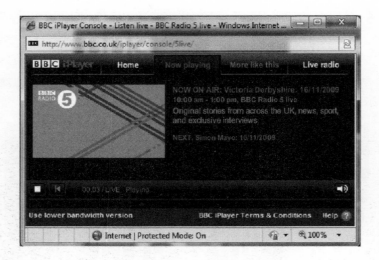

*you click on the one you want to listen to. You can
also use the search box at the top of the page.*

7 *When you are using the 'listen-again' service it is possible to move to different parts of the programme using the slider bar. Click and hold on the slider and move it across. It will show you in minutes how far through you are. Notice that you can also pause and rewind the programme.*

8 *You can leave the radio station playing and now go off and do other things on the Internet by opening a new tab in Internet Explorer.*

9 *When you have finished, click on the cross to close the website. You will get a message asking you to confirm that you want to close down.*

Another useful feature of Internet radio, which the BBC use, is to categorize by topic or musical taste. For example, if you like comedy programmes or jazz music, you might find programmes you want to listen to on Radio 2, Radio 3 and local radio stations. You can browse for individual programmes you might want to listen to regardless of what station they are on. To do this:

1 *Get back to the main BBC radio page at www.bbc.co/radio.*

2 *Select the music or speech type that you are interested in, e.g. Comedy. Notice that there is also an A–Z option here if you know the name of the programme you want to listen to. A new window will open that lists all the BBC programmes that feature comedy.*
3 *Click on the one you want and it will play the programme using the 'listen-again' feature described earlier.*

23.3 Watching TV

If you type 'Internet TV' into a search engine you will find that there are thousands of online TV stations to choose from. Some are free and some are a pay-per-view service. Many of these TV stations are the same ones you might find on satellite or cable TV. Like radio, the nature of the Internet means that some of the channels are quite specialized.

Online TV provided by the UK's main TV channels is a mixed bag. Some channels, like Channel 4 have an 'on-demand' facility where you watch particular Channel 4 programmes. This is called '4OD'. On-demand services are offered by some of the other big channels too.

Other websites offer a 'watch again' feature for some of their programmes, but usually only for a limited time after the programme was shown on normal TV. Some websites will offer snippets or trailers for TV programmes rather than the whole thing. The BBC for example offers a wide range of short video clips, including everything from news articles to exclusive behind-the-scenes videos. Some programmes are broadcast over the Internet at the same time that they are being broadcast on TV.

Hints and tips

Internet TV is one of the fastest changing areas on the Internet so it is worth looking on the website of your favourite broadcasters from time to time to see what's new.

However you access Internet TV you will watch it through a special piece of software called a **media player**. There are lots of players to choose from. The BBC's iPlayer is one example. Other websites have their own players and you can also use Windows Media Player or Real Player which are available to use on their own and not via a website.

Media players have some standard features most of which are the same as you might get on a normal CD or DVD player. As an example, we will look at Windows Media Player.

Open Windows Media Player by clicking on the icon in the Taskbar as shown.

Media players will pay audio and video and the controls are the same for each. In Windows Media Player they are the bottom:

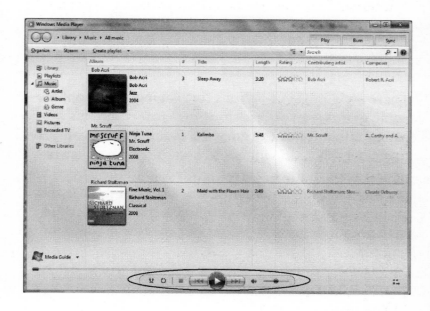

These are standard controls, and are similar to those on your video or DVD player. These are:

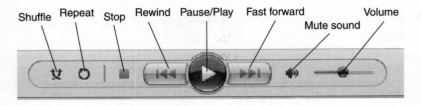

23.4 Online games

The intention of this section is not to show you any specific games, but to give some general advice on online gaming.

There are a range of options for playing games online. Some games sites are just for fun. Most computer games fall into this category, for example, you can play cards, scrabble, dominoes or chess. You can either play online against other players or download the game from the Internet onto your computer. Many of these games are free, but you may have to buy some of them. You may need to register with the website before they let you play.

Hints and tips

You need to be careful when downloading free games. It is possible to pick up viruses this way. If in doubt, get your games from a reputable and legal site.

There are also sites where you can play traditional gambling games like cards, roulette and bingo either against the computer or against other online players. You can potentially win (or lose) lots of money on these websites. These sites require you to register and you will also need to put into your credit/debit card details as you are playing for real money. Most sites ask you to deposit funds where you put a set amount of money in before you start playing. This way you can only gamble up to a certain limit.

To find games sites, use a search engine and type in the games that you are looking for. Alternatively, many well-known companies, such as the national bingo clubs, have websites where you can play gambling games online.

IMPORTANT THINGS TO REMEMBER FROM THIS CHAPTER

1 *The Internet has become a very popular way of accessing multimedia content, including music, videos, TV and games.*

2 *There are hundreds of online radio stations, including ones that you can also listen to on a traditional radio.*

3 *Online radio stations are available covering all possible genres including different types of music and talk radio.*

4 *You can listen to radio stations live or use a 'listen-again' feature to hear programmes you have missed.*

5 *Radio stations are usually played through a media player which is a piece of software designed to play multimedia files.*

6 *Using the media player you have some control over a programme. For example you can pause it and you may be able to rewind and fast forward.*

7 *There are loads of online TV stations covering a range of genres, many of which are available online.*

8 *Terrestrial TV stations do not normally broadcast their programmes online while they are going out live, but they do have a 'watch again' feature.*

9 *There are thousands of websites dedicated to playing games online.*

10 *Some games websites are traditional computer games and are free. Others are where you play against other online players, sometimes for real money.*

24

Accessing music and films

In this chapter you will learn
- *how to download and listen to music and audio books*
- *how to download and listen to podcasts*
- *how to use the Internet to buy CDs and DVDs*
- *how to rent films over the Internet*

24.1 Introduction

The Internet has roughly 1 billion users throughout the world. Anyone with a computer and an Internet connection can become part of the network. This represents a massive market for businesses and one of the big areas for them is music, audio and video. What this means is that however obscure your musical or film tastes, you will be able to find it somewhere on the Internet.

Another advantage is that you can get access to the music and videos that you want almost instantly as you can download it straight onto your computer. You don't have to go to the shops and you don't have to wait for delivery.

A disadvantage is that a lot of the music and films that can be downloaded are on websites which are not legally entitled to offer them, because they do not have copyright permissions. The difficulty is knowing which sites are legal and which are illegal. If you are downloading a feature film for free, and it's not some kind of special offer, then it is probably illegal. It's not so clear with music, where many artists make their work freely available online, hoping that this will encourage fans to buy their CDs and come to their shows.

One other factor we will cover in this chapter is that you can also use the Internet to buy traditional CDs and DVDs from online stores. We will also look at DVD rental sites, which are the modern equivalent of a video shop, with the added advantage that you don't have to leave the house.

24.2 Downloading music

Some music is available for free over the Internet, but most legal sites will charge you to download. Some sites charge you per track, while some charge a monthly amount and you are given set limits to how many downloads you can have. There are hundreds of download sites to choose from and a quick Internet search will list these for you. Some download sites require the use of special software, which you have to download. With others, you can do the download direct from the website. We will be looking at www.play.com, which does not require any specialized software.

You can download music and listen to it on your computer, or you can transfer it to an MP3 player. Some download sites also offer audio books as well as music.

Hints and tips

MP3 players are small portable devices used to play music. The 'MP3' comes from the type of computer file that is used to store music.

1 *Type www.play.com into the address bar of Internet Explorer.*
2 *Click on the link to 'MP3 downloads'.*
3 *Because a lot of younger people download music, often the first thing you see on these sites are lots of adverts for noisy music. Don't worry, there are all different types of music available. You've got two options for finding it. In common with other websites you have used, you can browse or you can search.*
4 *If you know the exact piece of music or artist that you are looking for, type the track name or artist into the search box at the top of the page and press the ENTER key. This example shows a search for Frank Sinatra. All tracks available on this site matching the search words are then shown.*

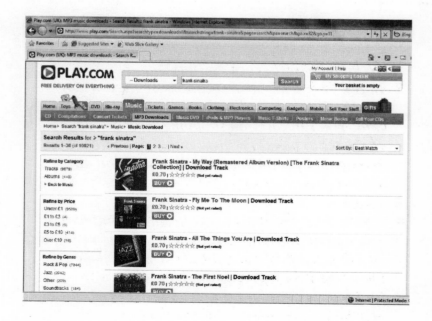

5 *To hear a brief sample, double click on the song title and then click on 'Play sample'.*

6 *To buy the track, click on 'Buy'.*

7 *In common with other websites where you buy things, there is a basket that the music track goes into. You can carry on shopping or go to the checkout to pay. The slight difference here is that you are not buying a physical product but an electronic download.*

8 *Click on 'Checkout'.*

9 *You will be prompted to create an account where you will be asked for the usual details about yourself and your bank account details. You can then use these every time you log onto this site.*

10 *You are then prompted to 'Confirm order'. Again, this process is very similar to buying any other type*

*of product from the Internet. The difference now is
that you will be prompted to download the track,
rather than waiting for something in the post.*

11 *Follow the instructions on screen and the download
will begin.*

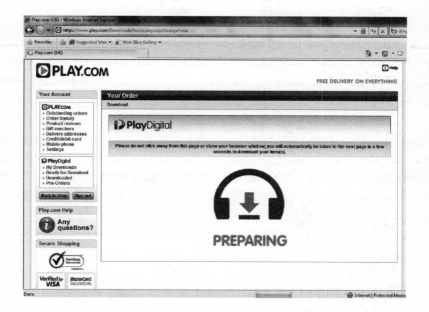

12 *If you do buy a track, it will take a short while to
download. If you are buying several tracks it will
take longer.*

13 *When it has finished, click on 'Open' and the track
will play using whatever media player is set up as
the standard setting on your computer.*

14 *When the track has finished downloading, click on
'Save' and save the track to your music library.*

You can listen to the track at any time either by
opening the Music library and double clicking on it or

by opening the media player, going to the Music library and clicking on it.

24.3 Podcasts

Podcasts are self-contained media (audio and video) files that are distributed by subscription. This means that you subscribe to a particular podcast site and it will download the latest instalment (called an episode) every time you log on. Podcasts are available from lots of different sites. Some are free subscriptions and you have to pay for others. Examples of popular podcasts might be those produced by radio DJs or TV presenters, who put together podcasts purely for entertainment purposes. Another use is for learning a language where each episode is a short lesson.

As with anything else on the Internet, a quick Internet search will throw up thousands of sites that you can look at. You do need to be quite specific with your search words in order to find what you want. In this

example, we will listen to and then download a podcast
from the Classic FM radio station.

1 *Type www.classicfm.co.uk/ into the address bar in
Internet Explorer.*

2 *Follow the links to 'Podcasts' or type 'podcasts' into
the search box.*

3 *Select the podcast that you want to listen to.
Note that there is a 'Listen now' option and a
'Download' option.*

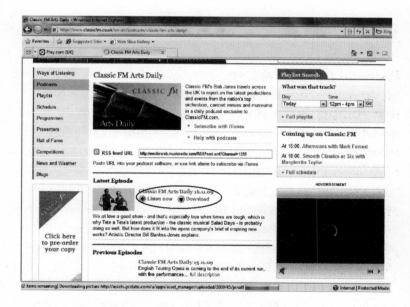

4 *As with a download that you pay for, you need
to save this podcast into your Music library or a
suitable playlist using your media player.*

24.4 Buying CDs and DVDs from online stores

The one disadvantage of downloading music and video onto your computer is that you have to sit in front of your computer to watch it, or copy it onto a CD or DVD so that you can play it on your normal equipment. Also, many people still like to buy a CD or DVD as they like to own the physical product, with the sleeve notes and all the extras.

If you are one of those people, the Internet can help you here too as there are lots of sites where you can buy CDs and DVDs and then have them delivered. Many of the businesses that do this are Internet-only and are able to offer lower prices. You will also be able to find an enormous selection of music and films, even if it is obscure or old.

The process of buying online is the same here as it would be for any other online purchase – you find what you want, order it and put your delivery address and credit/debit card number in. This example will use the same website that we used for downloads, Play. com, although there are lots to choose from, including websites run by well-know high street music retailers.

1 *Type www.play.com into the address bar of Internet Explorer.*
2 *You can now browse the site by following the various links, or if you know what you are looking for, you can type it into the search box.*

3 *In this example, a search is done for the film* Gone with the Wind *in the DVD section.*

4 *You can now click on any of the links to find out more about the DVDs. There are often several versions of the same film available in different formats. When you have chosen the one you want, click on 'Buy'.*

5 *If you want to buy more CDs or DVDs you can carry on searching and adding things to your basket. When you have finished shopping, click on 'Checkout' and you can pay.*

6 *As with all online shops, you need to register with the site. Most sites now use your email address as the user name and you then choose a password. Registering may take a few minutes, but once you have done it, it will remember your details for next time you buy something.*

24.5 DVD rental

A fairly new Internet idea is the online DVD rental website. Once registered you create a wish list of films that you would like to watch. The DVD rental company then sends them to you one-by-one using the good old-fashioned postal system. You watch them and send them back by post. When they get the DVD back, they send you the next one on the list and so on.

You pay a monthly fee for this that varies depending on how many videos you want at any one time. If you work it right it means that you will have a constant supply of DVDs to watch. They have thousands of DVDs to choose from including everything from the latest blockbuster films through to more obscure foreign films and all of the old favourites.

Hints and tips

Online DVD rental shops tend to have a much wider range than a normal video shop, and this includes all of the old classics. It's a great way to get hold of older films that you wouldn't normally find in a video shop.

There are a few sites to choose from and many large companies have got involved including Tesco, Blockbuster, Amazon, EasyCinema, Virgin and LoveFilm. Most of them offer a free trial so you could register with more than one and choose the best one. This example will use LoveFilm:

1 Type *www.lovefilm.com* into the address bar of Internet Explorer.

2 You need to register with the site before you can rent any films. You will be asked for delivery details and your credit/debit card details for payment. Once registered you will be able to log in with your email address and password.

3 You can now either browse or search. You can browse by clicking on the links near the top, or you can search by typing what you are looking for into the search box.

4 When you have found the movie you want you can usually do one of three things: buy it, watch it now (if available) or put it into your list of films that will be sent to you.

5 *As time goes by you will need to add further films
to your list. The 'Add to list' button changes to 'In
list – view' if it is already in your list. You can also
tick a box to remind yourself that you have already
seen a film.*

IMPORTANT THINGS TO REMEMBER FROM THIS CHAPTER

1 *Digital content, such as music and films, can be downloaded from the Internet.*

2 *There are a lot of websites offering music and film downloads without the permission of the copyright owners. It is illegal to download this content.*

3 *Music can be downloaded and played from your computer or you can transfer it to a portable music player.*

4 *Most legal websites will charge you to download music, although some music is free. You pay for this in the same way as any other online purchase.*

5 *A podcast is a self-contained download that is part of a series. You can subscribe to them or download the episodes you want to hear.*

6 *Many radio stations and TV programmes have their own podcasts, which are condensed versions of the shows.*

7 *You can find podcasts on a range of topics. For example there are podcasts for learning languages, comedy programmes and political commentary.*

8 *There are hundreds of online retailers of films and music. Often you can buy CDs and DVDs online cheaper than you can in high street stores.*

9 *There are DVD rental businesses such as Lovefilm operating online. These will send DVDs by post.*

25

....

Dating online

In this chapter you will learn
- *how to find and register with an online dating agency*
- *how to search for potential dates*
- *how to contact potential dates*
- *how to set up your own profile*
- *how to stay safe*

25.1 Introduction

There are literally millions of people using the Internet for dating purposes. One of the biggest sites in the world is <u>www.match.com</u> which boasts 6.5 million members in the UK alone. That's a lot of fish in the sea! There are lots of dating agencies to choose from and some of them specialize in particular interest groups or age groups. A quick search for 'over 50s + dating agency' will provide you with plenty of possibilities.

They all work in a similar way:

> ▶ *You register your details with the website and create a personal profile*

- *The website stores the profiles of all the people who are registered*
- *You search for the type of person you are looking for*
- *The website shows you the profiles of everyone who is a possible match*
- *You make contact (usually via email) with individual people*
- *You establish a rapport using email, or maybe in chat rooms*
- *You meet, you fall in love and live happily ever after.*

25.2 Registering with a dating agency

Most dating websites will ask you to register your basic details with them, e.g. name and email address before you can start using their site. They will usually let you search through and view members' profiles for free to see if there is anyone that you are interested in. If you find someone you want to contact, you then need to subscribe to the dating agency in order to get the email address of that person.

Hints and tips

Dating agencies are commercial businesses and make their money by charging a subscription rate – usually around £12 to £20 per month.

Typically you might find that there are several people you want to contact, and once you are a subscriber, you will be able to get the email addresses of any individuals that you are interested in.

We are going to use Match.com as an example. All dating agencies will work in a similar way.

1 *Type www.match.com into the address bar of Internet Explorer.*
2 *Fill in the details on the first page and click on 'Continue'.*

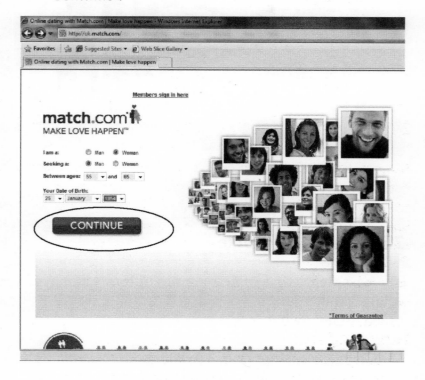

3 *You are now asked for some more information including the name that you want to be known by when using Match.com, an email address and password, and your postcode.*
4 *Complete the details and click on 'Registration completed'.*

25.3 Creating a profile

The next step is to complete a series of forms filling in
details about yourself, your ideal date and a section
called 'In my own words'.

1 *Complete each section. You will need to scroll
down to fill in all the boxes, and then click on
'Save and Continue' after each page. There is
quite a lot of information to fill in including
everything from your body size to your favourite
colour. You do not have to fill in every detail
if you don't want to as many of the questions
are optional.*

2 *When you have completed all the sections, which may take some time, you can 'Publish your profile'. At this point your details will be shown to anyone who is registered with the website.*

3 *You now have the option of uploading a photograph. To do this, you must already have one on your computer. Click on 'Upload photo' and find the photograph you want to use. If you don't want to add a photo just yet, click on 'Cancel'. You can add one at a later date.*

4 *Most dating websites allow you to register your details and search through other people's details for free. If you want to make contact with anyone you then need to subscribe and pay your monthly*

fee. By subscribing you can then get access to the email addresses of your potential matches so that you can contact them and establish a rapport. You can do this now or later on after you have searched through some of the potential matches.

5 *Subscribing is a similar process to any other purchase you make on the Internet in that you need to give them your card details. Make sure that you are happy with the contractual terms before you sign up. Most dating sites require you to sign up for a minimum period.*

6 *To get back to your profile at any time, click on the link to 'My profile' as shown. You can view and edit your profile here and upload photos.*

7 *To view your current matches, click on 'My Match'. More on this later.*

25.4 Searching for potential matches

1 *Click on 'Search'.*

2 *You can now search for possible matches by filling in some basic details. This should already have the settings that you put into when you first started using the site. Check the details are what you want and click on 'Search Now'.*

3 *You can experiment with some of the search options here and do this a number of ways depending on how picky you want to be. For example, you could*

search for all men within a 10-mile radius of where
you live. Or you could be more specific and search
for men aged between 55 and 60, who live within
10 miles and don't smoke, and have blond hair and
are 5ft 8in exactly! As you will see, the personal
profiles are very detailed, so you can search for very
particular characteristics if you want to.

4 In this example, the search is for men aged 50 to
65 who live within 50 miles of LE1 1AA. Click on
'Search now'. All of the people who match your
criteria are now listed. This particular search has
produced 10 pages of results, all of which have 16
different profiles. So that's 160 potential dates!

5 *You can scroll through the profiles looking at
the photos. If you see someone you like, click on
the photograph. This will open the profile of this
individual. As you can see the profile is very detailed
and covers everything from physical characteristics
to past relationships and lifestyle.*

6 *You need to take the time to read the profile, scrolling down, as there is quite a lot of it. You can go back to the results page and look through as many profiles as you like. Also notice that there is a link to 'See more like him' to find other people with similar characteristics. There is also a 'favourites' system like the one in Internet Explorer, so that you can save profiles and come back to them later.*

7 *If you want to carry out a more specific search, click on 'Search' at the top of the screen. You can now select very specific criteria to search on, e.g. people who are widowed or divorced and who don't smoke.*

8 *When you have put in your search criteria, click on 'Search now'. The results page will only show people who match your specific criteria. Bear in mind that the more specific the search, the less people you will get.*

9 *You can now look through and view the profiles of these people as described before.*

25.5 Getting in touch and staying safe

If you find people that you want to get in touch with, then initially this is done through email. You have to subscribe at this point if you want to get the email addresses of people you want to contact.

1 *To get an email address you click on the link at the bottom of the profile page of the person you are interested in.*

2 *People may also be contacting you having read your profile. To see if anyone has contacted you, click on 'My Match' at the top of the page and it will show you if you have any emails yet. If you have you can then respond to these people, if you want to.*

Up to this point, everything has been fairly anonymous, but once you get an email address, it starts to become more personal as you can begin an online conversation, which can develop in any direction you like. You may simply email each other and maintain an online relationship, or you may arrange to meet in an online

chat room, or even exchange phone numbers and talk over the phone. If things go well, you may arrange to meet for real.

Obviously there is some risk attached to this as you are meeting people that you don't know and you need to exercise some caution. Most online dating services take personal security very seriously, as in this case. Match.com provide quite a lot of information on safety.

3 *To read the safety information click on 'Help' at the top of the screen, and then follow the link to 'Safety advice'. There is also a 'How to report a user' feature if you are worried about anything that happens online.*

The main tips for safety are:

When **online:**

- *Stay anonymous until you feel confident enough to reveal your identity*
- *Use sensible email names and user names, i.e. nothing provocative*
- *Be honest in your personal profile and use a recent picture*
- *Report anyone who is abusing the system*

When **offline:**

- *Find out as much about them as possible before you meet*
- *Arrange to meet in a public place*
- *Tell a friend where you are going*
- *Make your own travel arrangements*
- *Watch your alcohol intake*
- *Don't be pressured into anything.*

On the whole dating online is a fun and safe activity. Basically you just need to use your common sense as you would in any other aspect of your life. The best advice is to trust your instinct.

IMPORTANT THINGS TO REMEMBER FROM THIS CHAPTER

1 *There are millions of people around the world using the Internet as a way of meeting new people.*

2 *Online dating agencies work in a similar way to real-world agencies in that you register your details and preferences, then find your ideal partner by browsing through their profiles.*

3 *You have to register with the dating agency websites. This includes your bank details as they make a charge for their services.*

4 *You are asked to complete a fairly detailed profile although you can give as much or as little information as you like.*

5 *Your personal profile details your own characteristics and tastes and any photographs you want to add.*

6 *You can search for potential dates using a range of criteria. For example those within a specific area, or with particular characteristics.*

7 *You can read through profiles of potential dates, then obtain their email address from the website and start making contact.*

8 *At the same time, people will be looking at your profile and may contact you.*

9 *You can take this contact as far as you like. You do not have to meet in the real world if you think that the person does not sound suitable.*

10 *You should exercise the same level of common sense that you would with any meeting that you arrange.*

Websites for the over 50s

In this chapter you will learn
- *how to find sites of specific interest to the over 50s*
- *how related websites are linked together*
- *how to use a portal website to link to other sites*

26.1 Introduction

The days when the Internet was for computer nerds and youngsters are well and truly over. A third of the UK population is now over 50 and more and more of the content of the Internet is now being targeted at this age group.

The idea of this chapter is NOT to give step-by-step guidance on how to access all of these websites but to list sites that might be of interest. Some of these sites have been designed specifically for the over 50s and some of them are designed for everyone to use, but will be of particular interest to the over 50s.

By now you will probably be quite used to searching the Internet, opening pages and following links and switching between pages. This chapter will be a good chance for you to put these skills to the test!

26.2 Portal websites

A **portal** is a particular kind of website that acts as a starting point for someone who is looking for information on the Internet. Portal sites usually have a particular theme. For example, there are many websites that call themselves 'portal sites for the over 50s'. This means that their website contains lots of information and lots of links to other websites that are of interest to the over 50s. If you can find a good portal site it can save you hours of Internet searching, because the portal website has already done the searching for you and listed useful sites in one place.

An example of a portal site, that we have already used in this book is www.directgov.uk, which is created by the UK government. As well as providing lots of information on public services, it also acts as a link to many other public services websites. On its home page, you can see all of the links. Some of these links are to other pages on this site, but many of them will be links to pages on other websites.

You can find over 50s portal sites by typing 'over 50s + portal' into a search engine. Here is a typical example from www.myprime.co.uk, which contains information and links specifically for the over 50s.

Follow the link to Directory, which in turn contains links to hundreds of other sites. These are categorized by topic, or you can click on their 'hot links', which will show you some of the most popular links that other people have used.

Other portal sites include:

- *www.50connect.co.uk*
- *www.mabels.org.uk*
- *www.retirement-matters.co.uk*
- *www.seniority.co.uk*

26.3 Links

You will find that websites often tend to have links to other related websites, even if they are not portal sites. For example, www.overfiftiesfriends.co.uk is an online community site where people can post profiles of themselves, join discussion forums and meet up locally in groups to take part in social activities. It also contains lots of links to other websites aimed at the over 50s. These links are to all sorts of sites including dating websites, other online community sites, and sites offering products and services for older people.

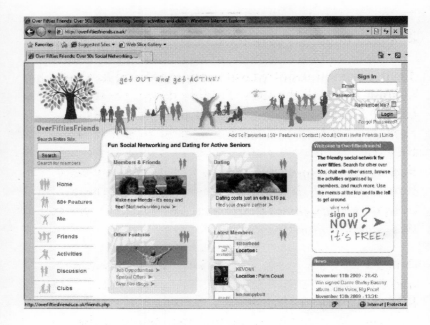

Once you find one good site, you will often find links to other good sites.

It is easy to lose track of which website you are in. Sometimes when you follow a link, it will open the web page in a new window. To get back to where you started you will need to click on the cross to close the new website. Sometimes the link will move you onto the new web page. You can use the Back button in Internet Explorer to move you back to where you started.

Hints and tips

Don't forget to add sites to your 'favorites' if you think that you will be using them regularly.

26.4 Choosing websites

There are millions of websites out there and new ones coming along all the time. Finding decent websites can be difficult. You can use a **search engine** to find sites, or you can ask family and friends what sites they use. Many of the national newspapers often print lists of useful websites, and it is possible to buy web directories, a bit like Yellow Pages (although these can go out-of-date quickly). You can also get website directories on the Internet.

When you are viewing websites it is worth thinking about who owns the site and why they have it. Sometimes it's hard to tell who owns a website and why they have put it on the Internet. Many of the websites we have looked at have been from government organizations or charities. Most are owned by commercial businesses and their motive is primarily to get you to buy something, so it doesn't hurt to be a bit sceptical at times.

Most websites tell you on their home page who they are and what they do. If it is not clear, try and find a link to 'About Us', which most sites have. There may be a main link to it or you may have to go to the bottom of the home page. The 'About Us' should tell you who owns the site and what kind of organization it is.

This is the 'About Us' page for www.fiftyon.co.uk which is listed later on.

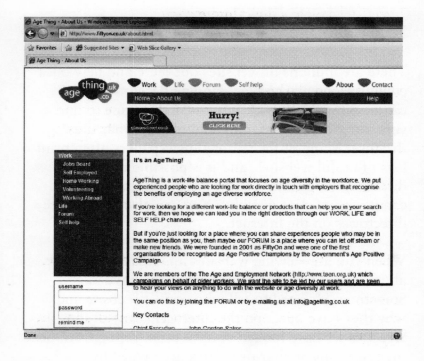

This makes it quite clear who is responsible for the site, and why they are running it.

26.5 Websites of interest to the over 50s

This section lists a small selection of websites that you might find useful, with a brief explanation of who owns the website and what it has on it. We have tried to focus on general sites that in turn will contain links to more specialized interests.

http://silversurfers.digitalunite.com/
Information relating to Silver Surfers week, which is run by Age Concern.

www.ageconcern.co.uk
The main website of the charity. Contains useful information about visual and audio aids when using computers.

www.wiseowls.co.uk
Information, advice and campaigns for the over 50s.

www.nhsdirect.nhs.uk/
Access to the services of the National Health Service.

www.saga.co.uk/
Company specializing in products and services for the over 50s.

www.dlf.org.uk/
Website of the disabled living foundation.

www.bbc.co.uk/health/health_over_50/index.shtml
Pages from the BBC website specifically about health for the over 50s.

www.fiftyon.co.uk
Website primarily concerned with employment issues for the over 50s.

www.lifes4living.co.uk/
Online community website for the over 50s.

<u>www.seniorconcessions.co.uk</u>
Website that searches for discounts available for older people on a range of products and services.

<u>www.theoldie.co.uk</u>
Website of the *Oldie* magazine.

<u>www.begrand.net</u>
Website specifically for grandparents.

IMPORTANT THINGS TO REMEMBER FROM THIS CHAPTER

1 *The over 50s represent a very large proportion of the total population. Consequently there is a lot of information on the Internet targeted at the age group.*

2 *A 'portal' website is one which is set up on a particular topic that contains links to lots of other related websites.*

3 *The government makes a lot of information available to the public via websites. Many of these are of particular interest to the over 50s.*

4 *There are a number of over 50s portal sites listed here and you are likely to come across many more when you are searching the Internet.*

5 *Portal sites might be set up by private companies, voluntary organizations or the government.*

6 *The Internet is home to many online communities. These are often organized by particular topics or in many cases by age.*

7 *Even if you have quite specific tastes, you will probably find communities on the Internet that are dedicated to it!*

8 *You will come across loads of websites when you are searching the Internet. To check they are reliable you can look at the 'About Us' page to see who is behind the websites and what their motives are.*

9 *Most websites exist to try and sell us something. You should exercise the same caution dealing with people online as you would in real life.*

10 *A number of websites of particular interest to the over 50s are listed in this chapter although this represent a tiny proportion of what is out there.*

Glossary

The numbers after the definition refer to the chapters in which the term is used.

address A way of identifying websites and emails (9)

address bar The place in a browser where you type in a web address, e.g. www.hodder.co.uk (4, 9, 10, 14)

address book An option in email software where you can store lists of email addresses (8)

adware/spyware Malicious software that sets itself up on your computer when using the Internet (3, 10, 16)

attachment Any file that is sent along with an email, e.g. a photograph (7)

backup A separate copy of your work usually saved onto a CD or DVD (16)

basket Container for what you have selected when you are shopping on the Internet (20)

blog A diary or journal on the Internet (14)

blogger Someone who writes a blog (14)

blogging The process of writing a diary or journal on the Internet (14)

broadband High speed access to the Internet (1, 11)

browse A method of looking through information, usually by category (3, 9, 19, 23)

browser Software for looking at websites (3, 9)

browsing The process of viewing web pages (3, 9, 19, 23)

CD-R A CD that can have information saved onto it once (16)

CD-RW A CD that can have information saved onto it over and over again (16)

chat room A place on a website where you can have online conversations with other people (5, 12)

computer system The generic term for a combination of hardware (equipment) and software (programs) (1, 3)

cursor The small vertical line that flashes on the screen to show you where the text will go when you start typing (4, 6)

dead link A hyperlink from a web page that does not lead to anything (9)

desktop the workspace in Windows – shows all the icons for the programs and folders on your computer; also, a type of computer that sits on the desk (as opposed to a laptop) (4)

device Generic term for any piece of equipment that you can plug into a computer (1, 3)

digital channels Radio and TV stations that are only available in digital format, i.e. through the Internet, digital TV, or DAB radio (22)

download The process of getting something from the Internet onto your computer (1, 9, 11, 15, 22, 23)

DVD-R A disk that can have information saved to it once (16)

DVD-RW A disk that can have information saved to it over and over again (16)

eBay An online auction site (19)

email attachment see attachment (7)

email address A unique name that you use when emailing, e.g. marjorie.franklin@googlemail.com (6, 8, 19)

email provider The business that provides you will access to email, e.g. Yahoo, BT, Tiscali, Microsoft (5)

favorites (favourites) A method of storing web addresses for quick access at a later date (10)

file All information stored on the computer is stored in files, so a file could be a document, a slideshow, a photograph or any other kind of information (4, 7, 8)

file-sharing Websites that allow you to share file (usually music or video) with other people – often illegally (15)

filtering and blocking software Software that prevents certain websites from being viewed (15)

firewall A method of stopping hackers getting access to your computer when you are on the Internet (15)

flatbed scanner A device for copying printed documents and turning them into a computerized version (1)

floppy disk A device for storing information

folder A place where files are stored on your computer, e.g. My Documents (4, 6, 7, 8)

forum An online message board (13)

gigabytes (GB) A measure of how much information can be stored on a computer (1, 2)

gigahertz (Ghz) A measure of the speed of a processor (1)

hacking Where someone gains unauthorized access to your computer – usually when you are on the Internet (15)

hard disk A device inside the computer where all information is stored (1)

hardware All the physical parts of a computer (1)

highlighted Shows when some text or an image has been selected (6, 10)

history file A record of the websites you have visited (10)

hits In a search engine, this shows the number of websites that are found when you type in some key words (9, 17, 18, 20, 21)

home page The first page of a website that usually contains an introduction to the website and lots of hyperlinks to other parts of the site (4, 9, 25)

host A computer that stores websites, usually owned by big computer companies like Yahoo or Google (13)

Hotmail The brand name of a web-based email service

hyperlink A link from a web page that leads to other web pages (5, 9)

icons Small pictures used to represent different things (4, 6, 7)

identity theft When someone pretends to be you with the intention on stealing from you (15)

Inbox Where messages are stored in email (6)

ink cartridges Replaceable unit placed inside an inkjet printer that contain the ink (1)

inkjet A type of printer that uses ink cartridges (1)

install The process of adding new software or hardware to the computer (11, 12)

instant messaging software A program that lets you have online conversations with other people (12)

Internet Explorer Software used to browse the World Wide Web. It is the brand name of Windows' Internet browser program (4, 10)

IP address The unique number that is assigned to your computer when you are on the Internet (15)

Internet Service Provider (ISP) The company that provides you with access to the Internet, e.g. Tiscali, AOL, Virgin etc (1)

iTunes Software used for downloading and organizing music from the Internet (7, 23)

jpg A file format for photographs and other images (7)

keyboard A device used to type into the computer (1)

kilobits per second (Kbps) A unit of measurement for data transfer, such as Internet connection speeds (1)

laser A type of printer (1)

link See hyperlink

log on The process of gaining access to a computer, or to websites. Usually involves typing in a password (18, 20)

maximize Making a window fill the whole screen (4, 6, 8)

media player Software for playing music and video (22)

megabits per second (mbps) A unit of measurement for data transfer, such as Internet connection speeds (1)

megabytes (MB) A measure of how big the computer's memory is (1, 2)

megapixel The unit of measurement used for digital cameras (2)

memory card A small plastic device inserted into a digital camera that stores the photographs (2)

memory stick A device that plugs into the computer and can be used for storing information (2)

menu The words across the top of the screen in software that let you get at the various options. Menus also appear when you right click (4, 6)

minimize Closing a window but leaving it available in the Taskbar (4)

modem A device needed for connecting your computer to the Internet (1)

mouse A device used to point and click on things on the screen (1)

mouse pointer The small arrow on the screen that can be controlled by moving the mouse (9)

multimedia Anything that combines text, graphics, sound and video (14, 23)

newsgroup A way of posting and reading messages on the Internet – organized into topics (13)

offline Using your computer when it is NOT connected to the Internet (24)

online Using your computer when it is connected to the Internet (12, 24)

online banking Doing your banking on the Internet (18)

online community People with a shared interest who communicate with each other over the Internet (14, 25)

online course Education or training that takes place entirely over the Internet (21)

online form The computer equivalent of a paper form that you need to fill in (5)

operating system Software needed to make your computer work, e.g. Windows XP, Vista, Windows 7 (1)

password A way of ensuring the correct person is using the computer (11, 15, 19, 20)

PayPal A method of paying for something that you have bought over the Internet (15)

peripheral Any piece of equipment that can be used in conjunction with your computer, e.g. a printer or scanner (2)

personal chat One-to-one conversation with someone you meet in a chat room (12)

phishing Where someone tries to get your bank account details from you via email, so that they can steal from you (15)

player See media player

playlist A collection of music (23)

podcast A self-contained voice, music or video broadcast delivered by subscription (23)

port A socket on your computer where something can be plugged in (1, 2)

post A comment added to a website or the act of putting a comment on a website (13, 14)

pop-ups Windows that appear (usually advertising something) when you are using the Internet (3, 16)

portal A website that provides links to other websites of a similar topic (25)

premium dialler Malicious software that connects your computer to the Internet at £1.50 or more each minute (15)

progress bar A window that shows you how long it is going to take for something to happen (16)

random access memory (RAM) Computer chips inside your computer that store programs and data (1)

real-time Something that is instant or 'as it happens' (12)

resolution The clarity of an image either on screen or printed (2)

restore Making a window bigger or smaller (4)

scanner See flatbed scanner (1)

scroll down Moving down a page (6)

scrolling The process of moving up, down or across a page (5, 24)

search A method of finding specific information when using the computer (9, 19)

search engine Software for searching the Internet (9, 10, 13, 14, 18, 21, 23, 25)

secure site A website that has extra protection for people making online purchases (15)

shortcut An icon, usually on the desktop that opens a program or folder (6)

shut down The process switching the computer off (4)

Skype The brand name of a company that provides Internet telephone calls (11)

social networking sites Websites where people put profiles of themselves and meet other people online (13)

software The programs that run on computers, e.g. Windows, Word etc. (1)

spam The email equivalent of junk mail (3, 6, 16)

sponsored links Links that are displayed in search engine results where the website owner has paid the search engine for the link to appear (17)

spyware/adware Malicious software that installs itself on your computer when you are on the Internet (3, 10, 16)

standard email software A program stored on your computer used for sending and receiving emails (5)

start-up routine The process that your computer goes through when you switch it on (4)

surf Informal term for the process of searching the Internet (9, 17)

tab Like a tab that you might get in an address book or folder dividers in real life, a tab is used to move to another page (10)

Taskbar The small bar at the bottom of the screen that shows which programs, folders and files are currently open (4)

toner Powdered ink contained within a replaceable unit placed inside an laser printer (1)

trojan A type of virus that is hidden inside another file (16)

updates Additions to software that provide new features (3)

upgrade The process of changing to the latest version of a piece of software (3)

URL An Internet address (14)

USB A method for connecting devices to your computer (1, 2)

USB port The socket on the front or back of the computer where you plug in a USB device (1, 2)

user name Required for some Internet services along with a password so that you can access them (11, 15, 19, 20)

virtual Term that covers anything that happens on the Internet (as opposed to happening in real life) (20)

virus Malicious software that installs itself on your computer and can cause damage to your data (3, 16)

virus checker Software that prevents viruses damaging your computer (3)

VOIP Voice over Internet Protocol – allows you to make telephone calls over the Internet using your computer (11)

web address The unique name used to identify a website (10, 21)

webcam A device that plugs into your computer and can be used to send moving images of yourself over the Internet (11)

web page A page of information on the Internet (9)

web-based A service that is provided over the Internet (5)

web-based email A service available on the Internet used for sending and receiving emails (5)

website Several pages of information on the Internet (9)

wiki A website where the visitor to the site can edit its content (13)

Windows desktop See desktop (4)

World Wide Web (www) The collective name for all the websites and web pages on the Internet (9)

worm See virus (16)

Index